W9-ARD-298

Asking them Questions
New Series
PART I

Also edited by Ronald Selby Wright

Asking Them Questions (1936)
Asking Them Questions, Second Series (1938)
Asking Why (1939)
Soldiers Also Asked (1943)
Asking Them Questions, Third Series (1950)
Asking Them Questions: A Selection from the
    First Three Series (1953)
Fathers of the Kirk (1960)
A Manual of Church Doctrine according to the
    Church of Scotland (with T. F. Torrance, 1960)

By Ronald Selby Wright

Take Up God's Armour (1967)

Asking them Questions

New Series

PART I

'They found Him . . . sitting in the
midst of the doctors, both hearing
them, and asking them questions.'
LUKE 2:46

EDITED BY

Ronald Selby Wright

CARNEGIE LIBRARY
LIVINGSTONE COLLEGE
SALISBURY, N. C. 28144

LONDON
OXFORD UNIVERSITY PRESS
New York   Toronto

Oxford University Press, Ely House, London W.1

GLASGOW   NEW YORK   TORONTO   MELBOURNE   WELLINGTON
CAPE TOWN   IBADAN   NAIROBI   DAR ES SALAAM   LUSAKA   ADDIS ABABA
DELHI   BOMBAY   CALCUTTA   MADRAS   KARACHI   LAHORE   DACCA
KUALA LUMPUR   SINGAPORE   HONG KONG   TOKYO

ISBN 0 19 213423 X

© Oxford University Press, 1972

First published 1972
Second impression 1973

All rights reserved. No part of this publication may be reproduced, stored in a retrieval system, or transmitted, in any form or by any means, electronic, mechanical, photocopying, recording or otherwise, without the prior permission of Oxford University Press.

This book is sold subject to the condition that it shall not, by way of trade or otherwise, be lent, re-sold, hired out, or otherwise circulated without the publisher's prior consent in any form of binding or cover other than that in which it is published and without a similar condition including this condition being imposed on the subsequent purchaser.

Set I.B.M. by George Over Ltd, London and Rugby

Printed in Great Britain by

Fletcher & Son Ltd, Norwich

230
W952
c.2

Dedicated to

ALEK W. SAWYER

and

W. ROY SANDERSON

101186

Preface

The original series of *Asking Them Questions* owed its origin, as some readers may remember, to questions asked me by the then members of my Boys' Club, most of whom had in these days no Church connection, came from poor homes, and few, if any, I thought had any kind of real interest in religion. When, as I got to know them better, we began to quite naturally discuss the meaning and purpose of life as we camped together or sat around the Club fire, I found that the interest was very much there and that the kind of questions they asked were of a nature that greatly surprised me and required much more serious and considered answers than I, a young raw student, felt competent to give. And so, as much for my own help as for theirs, I sent some of the questions to good and scholarly men and asked if they could help, beginning with two of my own most admired teachers, Professor H. R. Mackintosh and Professor A. E. Taylor. Their instant sympathetic response gave me the encouragement I needed to approach others; and to my great delight I found that most, too, readily agreed to help. Gradually the questions and answers began to accumulate, and feeling that they were too good to keep to ourselves, I then approached the Oxford University Press who, seeing their worth, agreed to publish them. The book's reception was quite surprising and it quickly went into nine impressions, four in its first year, and it also led to more questions being sent to me from all sources, not least from Headmasters and School Chaplains from many different parts of the United Kingdom and many from overseas.

A second series followed in 1938 which went into seven impressions, and a third in 1950; and in 1953 it was decided to make a *Selection* from the three series. (In 1943 a similar book was published called *Soldiers Also Asked* consisting of questions asked by those in H.M. Forces at Padres' Hours and was reprinted the following year.)

Visits to a large number of schools and my connection particularly with three schools in Edinburgh — Fettes College,

Loretto School and Edinburgh Academy — made me and many others realize the need now for a completely new series; and the schools themselves, largely through the Headmasters or Chaplains, sent in lists of questions that the boys or girls were actually asking; and here I would especially like to express my gratitude not only to the above schools, but to schools as varied in distance and composition as Eton, Felsted, Lancing, Rossall, Sedbergh, Sherborne, Wellington, and Winchester, and a number of Grammar and Comprehensive Schools throughout the country.

Many of the questions were understandably much the same, and these have, as far as possible, been covered in a comprehensive question; some were of such a contemporary nature as would quickly date them; by no means all were those asked by the original Club boys, and indeed there are some which in those days would never have crossed their mind — who, for example, would have thought of asking questions like 'When are we dead?' (included in Part II of this New Series) or questions on outer space and the permissive society (also in Part II) All the questioners were anonymous so that the questioners were free to ask what they liked, and all are genuine.

And it is surely right that we should ask questions. Were not the disciples themselves 'desirous to ask Him'[1] and Fr. Arthur Stanton of Holborn once said 'we are poor children crying for the light; but it is because we are children and we are alive that we long to ask the questions. Dead men never ask questions. It is because you are alive and your soul is alive and your heart is alive, . . . that you long to know that which is above and about you'.[2]

If this book has shown nothing else to me, it has shown that young people today are even more interested and concerned about belief and the meaning of life than were their fathers.

Each generation to some is never as good as the one before. Youth in one form or another is always 'revolting'. The criticism of young people today is much the same as it ever was . . . 'The world is passing through troubled times. The young people of today think of nothing but themselves. They have no reverence for parents and old age. They are impatient of restraint. They talk as if they alone knew everything, and what passes with us as wisdom is foolishness to them. As for the girls, they are immodest and unwomanly in speech, behaviour and dress.' But 'the young people of today' referred to are those in the year 1294, for the above was written by Peter the Monk! Or this as another example: 'I cannot suppose thee to be such a stranger in England as to be ignorant of the general complaint concerning the decay of the power of godliness, and more especially of the great corruption of youth. Wherever thou goest, thou wilt hear men crying out of bad children and bad servants; whereas indeed the source of the mischief must be sought a little higher: it is bad parents and bad masters that make bad children and bad servants; and we cannot blame so much their untowardness, as our own negligence in their education.' That was written by Mr. Thomas Manton in a prefatory letter to the Confession of Faith in 1643.

These quotations — and I could add others — have a strange contemporary ring about them. The 'good old days' exist largely in older people's imagination when summer holidays were always sunny; but personally I believe that far more true of today's generation are the words of Mr. Anthony Chenevix-Trench, the former Headmaster of Eton and now Headmaster of Fettes, who has said that 'the new generation is morally braver, more truthful, more serious, intelligent, candid and frank'. Bad news is so often 'good news' and the minority hit the headlines. We hear about the fifty students who break into a building but not about the nine thousand nine hundred and fifty who are getting on with their work; but it is the vast majority, so often forgotten, that 'maintain the fabric of the world'.[3] It is of course true that 'the young people of today' have in a moral and spiritual, though not in a material sense, a more difficult world to contend with than was the case when even the first series of *Asking Them Questions* appeared. They are faced with much more publicity — through radio, television and press; they have a greater opportunity for travel and certainly more 'freedom', and though there have always been temptations, for which we should be grateful — for without temptation character cannot be tested — the temptations today can be much more subtle and insidious, and many are such as were unknown a generation ago. But the eternal truths remain and with them still

> . . . those obstinate questionings
> Of sense and outward things[4]

though, of course, some of the 'outward things' of today have a rather different connotation from that which they had to Wordsworth.

There is one point that I mentioned in the Preface to the original series which I should like to underline again, and that is that no amount of knowledge about religion will ever make a man religious. To know about our Lord Jesus Christ is not the same thing as to know him.[5] Yet, is it not almost impossible to know anyone unless we know something about him? And no amount of argument can ever by itself convince a man. As Dr. Edwyn Bevan has so truly said, 'Argument, generally speaking in religion, can do no more than clear the track; it cannot make the engine move'.[6] But this is no reason for not helping to 'clear the track'. Faith, of course, there must ever be, and without it our religion is worth little. But the word 'faith', if we are not careful, can often become just another name for laziness; and the clever should not be confused with the wise. As Professor A. E. Taylor once put it, 'For all of us, the journey will have to begin with a venture of faith reaching out in a true humility of spirit to things which are not seen. Nor is this reasonable humility of mind to be disparaged as what our latest unlovely jargon calls "wishful thinking". For genuine "wishful thinking" we must turn to the kind of "agnostic" who "in the dark that covers" him blusters about his own "unconquerable soul", not to the Christian who says "not as though we were sufficient of ourselves . . . our sufficiency is of God".'[7] Our Lord studied the Scriptures, and as we have seen, asked questions. Dare we do less than follow his example? And can we do more than pray that his Spirit may be given to us as we earnestly seek after the truth, so that we may day by day, in our journey through life, try to become more like him?

Not all the papers included in this book are easy to understand; some require careful thought and help from older people; but it is not a bad thing for a young person to find that truth is not always easily comprehensible;[8] many things may be seen 'through a glass darkly':[9]

> . . . a man's reach should exceed his grasp,
> Or what's a heaven for?[10]

In other words, this book will never make a man a believer in the Christian faith and life against his will; but I do think it may help to clear away some of the stumbling blocks and show that the Christian belief, when tested by reason and tried out in life, will prove it is valid and is such that we may reasonably put trust in it.

I am grateful to Bishop Hugh Montefiore for permission to include his article and those by the Archbishop of Canterbury, Bishop Butler, and the Rev. H. A. Williams, which I have, by permission of the authors, adapted and edited, and the main content of which formed the basis of sermons preached by them at Great St. Mary's, the University Church, Cambridge, while he

was Vicar. And finally I would like to thank all those who have
made this book possible by contributing so willingly and so ably.
Of the first series, only seven of the forty contributors are, as I
write, still alive; and, a generation later, though so many of the
questions are basically still the same, the approach differs. Each
contributor is of course responsible for his own contribution only
and none would claim to give the final word, but each at least, I
hope, can set us thinking and talking and so get clearer the truth
we are all seeking. And I should like to thank, too, all those
others for the great help they have given — the Headmasters and
Chaplains already referred to, Mr. N. J. Wheatley, who has
compiled the Index, and also The Rev. Hugh Mackay, and my
secretary Mrs. Taylor: but I am especially grateful to Mrs. Joan
White and Mr. Geoffrey Hunt of the Oxford University Press for
their never-failing help, advice and encouragement.

In the first series, the work of forty contributors could be
included in one handy volume, because the contributions though
coming from eminent men were relatively short and simple, as
was then required to meet the needs of the questioners. In this
New Series, the ground covered by young people's questions is at
least as wide as before, and in order to meet difficulties fully and
fairly, the contributors have been given rather more scope. The
work was planned as a whole, but for the convenience of readers
it is being published in two volumes. Part I comprises questions
on the great fundamental subjects like the existence and goodness
of God, the inspiration of the Bible, miracles, Jesus Christ, his
birth, passion and resurrection, and the life after death. Questions
concerning the Holy Spirit, the Church, the earthly life of the
individual and society, and particularly problems of the modern
world, will be found in Part II, the publication of which follows
shortly after Part I. Details of the contents of Part II are given for
reference on pages 161—2 of this volume and the two Parts are
intended to complement each other. The Index of Contributors
(pages 163—7) covers both Parts.

Canongate   RONALD SELBY WRIGHT
Edinburgh
Michaelmas 1971

---

1 St. John 16:19.
2 *Faithful Stewardship* by Fr. Stanton (p. 73)
3 Ecclesiasticus 38:34 (AV has 'state of the world').
4 William Wordsworth, 'Intimations of Immortality'.

5   cf. St. John 5:39: 'You study the Scriptures . . . and yet you refuse to
    come to me for life!' (Jerusalem Bible).

6   Edwyn Bevan, *Hellenism and Christianity*.

7   A. E. Taylor, *Does God Exist?* (p. 171f)

8   I am indebted to Dr. A. L. F. Smith, as I write now, the oldest Fellow
    of All Souls and a former Rector of the Edinburgh Academy, for
    reminding me of a sentence from the late A. J. Balfour: 'A religion that
    is small enough for our understanding is not great enough for our need'.

9   I Corinthians 13:12 (or 'a dim reflection in a mirror', Jerusalem Bible).

10 Robert Browning: 'Andrea del Sarto'.

Contents

What is the purpose of life?

We cannot begin to get a satisfactory answer to the question: What is the purpose of life? until we have tackled the question: What is man? If to this latter question we give a purely materialistic answer, we shall approach the former question from an angle wholly different from that of the person who thinks of man as a spiritual being. What is man? A bundle of chemicals worth a few shillings in all? A body made up of a hundred billion or so cells? Will that do for an answer? I think not. 'Man is like unto the beasts that perish' — that is a Biblical answer, the reply of a Psalmist who was oppressed by the obviously transitory nature of life and whose understanding had not been illuminated by the Christian conception of life after death (Psalm 49:12). But that is only one answer — a depressing one — from the pages of the Old Testament. There are glimpses there, long before the coming of Jesus of Nazareth, of a more satisfying reply. Another Psalmist poses the question: 'What is man?' (Psalm 8:4). He sets it against the awe-inspiring background of a universe which puzzles him by its magnificence — 'When I consider thy heavens ... the moon and the stars'. He knows nothing of the immensities of time and space which we have begun to understand in recent centuries, but he knows enough to make him feel very small. We might imagine that he would reply: 'Man is nothing; a puff of wind, a spark soon exterminated.' But he gives a wholly different answer. 'Thou madest him little lower than the angels', he replies. 'Thou hast crowned him with glory and honour. Thou madest him to have dominion over the works of thy hands, and hast put all things in subjection under his feet, all sheep and oxen, yea and all the beasts of the field. ...' In other words, man, tiny and transitory as he is when compared with the immensities of the universes, is yet God's vice-gerent. He is to have dominion, the while he himself is under the dominion of God.

Now we are getting somewhere. If this is true, there inheres in man a certain *responsibility*, an answerability to God, which gives him a dignity unique in creation. The process of the evolution of *homo sapiens* is a mystery, and much of the story is still tentative. Professor L. C. Birch, in his book *Nature and God* (pp.36—7), has put it this way: 'Were it possible, by some act of necromancy, to resurrect our evolutionary forbears, and set them in a long line from earliest to latest, and then to review them as one might review a guard of honour, it is unlikely that we would be able to say: "Well, here at last is a man, the creature on his left is not." ' That is doubtless true. But what is it that constitutes the *humanum*, the distinctive characteristics of man? Is it not his ability to evaluate, to stand over against nature of which he is a part, and to fulfil his function of responsible domination over what has been entrusted to him?

The old creation story of Genesis 2 must not be dismissed as just another of the primitive stories of earth's origins which most primitive peoples have handed down. It has profound insights. When God had made man, he put him in the garden 'to dress it and to keep it'. So there is a dignity to labour. Man is responsible; he is entrusted with soil and plants and trees. Then God formed the beasts and the birds — the language is highly poetic and contrasts strangely with the picture which the scientists present to us. That does not matter. We must note what God does when he has made the animals. He brings them to Adam 'to see what he would call them: and whatsoever Adam called every living creature, that was the name thereof' (Genesis 2: 19). The point of this strange saying is this: If I know the name of a thing or an animal, still more if I give it its name, that thing or that animal is in my power. I am its master. So we see man as master of the animal world, God's vice-gerent as it were, having dominion over the beasts, but answerable to God for the kind of dominion which he exercises. Man is over Nature and under God. (In passing, one may be allowed to draw attention to what happens to our earth when there is no sense of responsibility, of *answerability* to God for being put in trust with nature. Dust-bowls and contamination of the atmosphere by atomic explosions are but two illustrations).

The story of the garden and the animals is followed by the story of the making of a companion for Adam. Again, the language is highly poetical. The point of the story is not far to seek. Man, if he is to be truly man, must live in harmony not only with Nature, plants and beasts, but in community with others like himself. Indeed, the opening three chapters of Genesis make it abundantly clear that if man is to become fully human, he must learn to live in a right relationship with God, with others, and with Nature. Thus man can rejoice in God, that is to say, he can live in community, he can develop as a son of the Most High, he can exercise his vice-gerency in humble responsibility.

The old Genesis story is reflected in a powerful sentence in Psalm 100 (v.2): 'Be ye sure that the Lord he is God: it is he that hath made us and we are his . . . '. This is taken up by the writer of the Epistle to the Ephesians (2:10): 'We are God's handiwork . . . '. The word is *poiēma*, which has been taken over into English as *poem*. A poem is the noblest expression of the poet's mind, his best expression of himself. That, so St. Paul suggests, is what man is intended to be, the finest flowering of God's mind within his creation. The tragedy of life lies in the fact that we, by our folly, spoil the metre and wreck the poem (and, incidentally, in doing so, grieve the Poet, who, if we follow the teaching of Jesus, is not only Artist but Father). Kierkegaard, the great Danish thinker, says that each man's life is to be a poem, as if we are each to write or compose ourselves. But a Christian allows God to write his life's poem; in so far as that takes place he reaches his full humanity and finds his purpose in living.

So we have moved from the question: 'What is man?' to our original question: 'What is the purpose of life?'

This is a question which presents itself to anyone who is at all serious about the business of being human. It has a way of teasing us, even when we are young. We can seek to stub it out, as a man puts out the fire at the end of his cigarette. We can seek to prevent its recurrence, as something too problematical to worry about. But in doing so, we cannot but feel that we are abandoning ourselves to a method of living which is unworthy of us. The question, even if, as is probably the case, it cannot be fully answered, must (to use the language of the examination room) be attempted.

Here am I, a mysterious entity of passions and desires, of hopes and fears, of possibilities for good and ill. I came on the scene only very recently, if you compare me with the physical world of which I am a part. I shall disappear from the scene very shortly — I may live to be 90 or 100, but that is a mere second in time if you think, as you must, in terms of a universe where millions of years are your standard of measurement. Can you speak of *purpose* for so tiny, so transitory, a thing as that?

I believe you can. I believe you *must* think in terms of purpose, if life is to have a thrust to it which delivers it from being a mere sharing in a succession of random events and then — out into the dark.

There is a wide variety of possibilities open to the man who is prepared to put the question to himself. For example, he may say: I am a bundle of desires which cry out for satisfaction. Hunger, thirst, sex, the whole world of sensation, are there to be fulfilled. The purpose of life, so far as I am concerned, is to see that these desires are met as they press their claims on my attention. Most thoughtful people would say that, legitimate as those claims are, important as is the place which man's hungers hold in his make-up, the satisfying of them as a main motive for living is an unworthy one. Even the satisfying of the desire for knowledge, if it be pursued simply for itself and not for the ultimate enrichment of mankind, can be a selfish thing.

What is the purpose of life? We cannot get far with this question without coming up against the profit motive. 'I want to make £100,000 before I am 35.' Good. Or is it? It may well be. It all depends on the motive behind the desire. Let me contrast two men of our own time, both of whom became immensely rich. Here is King Farouk of Egypt who amassed a huge fortune and lived in fabulous luxury, while the vast majority of his people lived around him in grinding poverty. He died at an early age largely owing to the dissipation of which he had become a victim. Or here is William Richard Morris, known to the world as Lord Nuffield. He began work, as everybody knows, in a little bicycle shop in Oxford. He ended life as a millionaire whose wealth has saved thousands of lives through the medical institutions which he founded and the research which he made possible. The profit motive, like ambition in general, is an a-moral thing. Everything depends on what you hitch your motive to.

Put our question to many seriously-minded men and women to-day, and they would reply: 'My purpose in living is to leave this world a better place than it was when I entered it.' That is good. I shall suggest later that it is not good enough, but, so far as it goes, it is good. It has provided the stimulus for a multitude of noble lives – and anything that does that cannot, must not, be airily dismissed. Life for multitudes of our contemporaries is a grim affair, a pitiless struggle for existence, a battle against elements which bid fair to destroy them. The so-called 'third world', the world of dire poverty, of illiteracy, of lack of amenities which we in the West take for granted as minimal necessities, this is the world in which tens of millions of our fellow-men eke out a short and miserable existence. To strike a blow against *that*, to pit our learning against that ignorance, to bring hope and a fuller life even to a comparative handful of people less fortunate than ourselves — *that* is to give a really meaningful answer to our question. A man who works on these lines may feel, at the end of his life, that that life has not been in vain. It has had purpose.

The Christian gives his whole-hearted assent to this answer to the question. But he goes further. Simply 'to leave the world a better place than it was when he entered it', good as that motive is, is not good enough for him. He has a higher point of reference. If he was born north of the Border, he is familiar with the answer to the question: 'What is the chief end of man?' which is given in the Scottish Shorter Catechism: 'The chief end of man is to glorify God and to enjoy him for ever.' We are back at the Poet and the poem. We are back at man's answerability which is the essence of his humanity. The Christian sees his purpose, in life in terms of his response to God. His attitude to persons is what it is because of his attitude to God who made them and him. He cannot treat them as things to be manipulated for his pleasure or profit. They are, as he himself is, children of God, designed to be his 'poems', capable of almost limitless growth. They must, therefore, be treated with reverence. If Jesus came that men 'might have life and have it in all its fullness' (St. John 10:10), then it will be the Christian's chief aim to forward that purpose. In that way, he will 'glorify God', and prepare for a fuller life when he will 'enjoy him for ever'. He will see life, with all its absorbing interest, in its relationship to the Creator, to his fellow-creatures, to Nature; and he will see it as a training-ground for life after death. That is the context of his living. Everything is *sub specie aeternitatis*. There is no limit to his horizons. The prospects are exciting.

With these horizons and prospects, with these terms of reference, and with this overwhelming sense of answerability, the Christian disciple will obviously be prepared for a life of self-discipline and training. The great ecumenical leader, Archbishop Nathan Söderblom, constantly used to avail himself of the metaphor of the race-horse and its rider in this connection. The good horse, he would say, can achieve its highest capacity and its greatest speed only under the sure hand of the rider. Kierkegaard, using the same language of the apostles, said that they were 'well broken in'. That is true of Christ's disciples at all times. Söderblom said: 'Only with God's good hand and strict bridle can the soul be helped to give its best.' (Bengt Sundkler, *Nathan Söderblom, His Life and Work*, p.152). He was right. To revert to our earlier metaphors, the vice-gerent exerts his sovereignty rightly only when he himself bows to the sovereignty of God. The poem attains its full power and beauty only when the Poet has a free hand to make of it what he will.

Literature is full of instances of men who have failed to see this, and because they have lacked this vision, have perished. A. J. Cronin, in one of his less known novels, *The Northern Light*, tells the story of the manager of a newspaper who sought to run it on lines which gave its readers the best kind of journalism and avoided the cheap and the salacious. The heart of the story is a take-over bid which Henry Page, the manager, resists. When it is seen that no offer is acceptable, a rival paper is started up in the town with the object in view of ruining *The Northern Light*. It very nearly succeeds — but not quite. The central figure of the opposition is one Leonard Nye. Cronin uses all his skill in describing him. It is not merely his cunning which stands out in the story. It is his closure of his heart to pity, his willingness to use people and to ruin them if by so doing he can achieve his aims, which make Nye so despicable a character. People are pawns in his little game of living. Only one person matters, Leonard Nye, his wealth, his aggrandisement. What matter if he leaves the world a *worse* place than he found it, so long as his own selfish aims are achieved? Cronin answers our question brilliantly in his character-sketches of Page and Nye. Page lives for the community. Nye has not begun to live in community; God does not exist in his thinking — there is no one to whom he is answerable for the use of his gifts. The centre of Nye's universe is Nye. His horizons are narrow, his prospects beyond this life are nil, his sense of answerability to God, if it ever existed, has died on him. He has lost his soul.

A. J. Cronin has provided us with an illustration of a man who had not a clue as to the real purpose of life. The New Testament shall provide us with two instances of those who had.

Saul of Tarsus is a good example of a man who 'changed horses in mid-stream'. All his considerable energies as a young man were devoted to persecuting the followers of Jesus of Nazareth. Then he met him and, yielding him his allegiance, spent the rest of his life in serving his cause and winning men to his service. His letters reflect this dramatic change and give us a vivid picture of a man quite clear as to the purpose of life. I choose two typical utterances. *First:* 'It is God himself who called you *to share in the life of his Son Jesus Christ our Lord*' (1 Corinthians 1:9). Here is human destiny at its highest. The men to whom St. Paul wrote knew a good deal about the life of Jesus Christ. Some, maybe, had seen him in the flesh and heard him. Many had listened to those who had lived with him in Palestine. All knew of the power and love of that life lived for others, a life which death by crucifixion had been unable to extinguish, a life which was available to them in prayer and sacrament. *Here*, precisely, for them was the purpose of life — 'to share in the life of the Son of God'.

Secondly: We make it our ambition to be well-pleasing to him' (2 Corinthians 5:9). The 'we' is editorial; this is clearly a statement of personal aim and ambition. We have seen earlier that ambition in itself is an a-moral thing — it all depends on what you hitch it to. Here it is a thing of immense moral power — every personal desire is subjugated to the overmastering ambition of pleasing Christ. This is the one passion of his life. This gives life its purpose and its meaning.

'Life' writes Stephen Neill 'is filled with meaning as soon as Jesus Christ enters into it. Man realizes himself to be part of a great purpose in which he can participate, and in which all his minor purposes can find place and significance. The knowledge of the ever-present Christ can reach down into the hidden depths and assure lonely modern man that he is not alone. More than that; it can draw him out of his loneliness to the rediscovery of the human race.' (*The Church and Christian Union*, p.279). That is not a bad summary, by a modern writer, of St. Paul's two statements: 'God . . . called you to share in the life of his Son Jesus Christ', and 'We make it our ambition to be well-pleasing to him.'

If St. Paul furnished us with our first instance of a man equipped with a clear purpose for living, a greater than St. Paul shall provide us with the second. I take two sentences from the Fourth Gospel, one of which I have already quoted.

First: 'I have come that men may have life, and may have it in all its fullness' (St. John 10:10). Here, quite clearly, is a life lived with no thought for self but wholly for others. The context shows that such a life involves sacrifice, even to death — 'the good shepherd lays down his life for the sheep'. And it involves battle; there are forces of evil represented by 'the thief' and 'the wolf' which must be opposed. The purpose of life depicted here is a stern one.

Secondly: 'I have made thy name known . . .' (St. John 17:6 & 26). These words are not purposive in their form, but, taken in their context, they declare the fulfilment of the purpose which Jesus saw as the meaning of life. They are taken from a long

chapter which purports to give us the prayer of Jesus at the end
of his earthly life, immediately prior to his self-sacrifice on the
Cross. He declares that that purpose was to 'make known the
name of God' to the men whom God has given him as his
immediate followers. It would then be for them in their turn to
continue to make his name known to others — so the knowledge
would spread in ever widening circles. The 'name' represented to
a Jew the *personality*. If one made another person's 'name'
known one drew aside the veil that hid him. One showed him for
what he essentially is. That is precisely what Jesus did. Before his
coming, men had a partial or a distorted or a warped view of God.
Many were tiring of the crude polytheism of the Hellenistic gods
and the emperor-worship of Rome. Many were looking wistfully
to the worship of the synagogue and were pondering on the
message of the prophets — the rigorous justice of an Amos, the
yearning love of a Hosea, the ethical rectitude demanded by the
God of Isaiah. Here were glimpses of a religion which could
satisfy the deepest longings of men both in their personal religion
and in their desires for a satisfying social ethic. And then Christ
came and, in coming, drew aside the veil that had partially or
almost completely veiled the Face of God, and men saw in him a
King to be obeyed, and a Father to be loved. Here was one
worthy of total response. To be the vice-gerent of such a
Sovereign was man's highest destiny. To exercise responsibility,
answerability, was to live life in all its fulness. To allow such a
Poet to create his poem without let or hindrance was to find life
that was life indeed.

> To know him is to live;
> To serve him is to reign.

I doubt whether we can go further than this, but this is enough
to begin to make sense of life and its purpose at least for me. The
unsolved mysteries of life are legion. The agnostic element in any
thoughtful man's philosophy of life must be great; he must be
prepared to say, again and again, 'I do not know'. 'My knowledge
now is partial' — St. Paul said that nineteen centuries ago and, for
all the strides which science has made, it is still true, for our
horizons are far wider than were his. But we know enough to see
that God has a purpose for the lives of his children and that he
has made us in such a way that we can enter into that
purpose — or spurn it.

I believe that a purpose is found for life when God is seen to
be constantly at work within his creation, God who is both

Sovereign Lord and loving Father; God who has spoken finally in Jesus his Son; God who was in Christ reconciling the world to himself; God who, by his Spirit, constantly seeks to make us holy, that is to say, to fashion us after the likeness of his Son. This God treats us as responsible beings, answerable to him for the response we make to his love shown in Christ, for the way we treat his sons and daughters, for our attitude to nature in its myriad manifestations. This God never forces our response — as Augustine said, he 'asks our leave to bless us'. But when that leave is given, he gets on with the making of his poem. Then, and only then, is the purpose of life achieved.

DONALD EBOR:

Who is God?

The trouble with many people who take a pride in calling themselves atheists is that they have not stopped to imagine who God is, what kind of being this is, whose reality and very existence they want to deny. In a way, it is not their fault altogether because large numbers of schools have stopped giving what used to be called religious instruction, and in those which do give it, many pupils choose to opt out. In fact 'opting out' is a not bad definition of atheism itself. To be fair to such people, those who call themselves Christian ought to be prepared to make a serious attempt to set down as clearly as possible their idea of who God is. So then in looking at this question we are not trying to offer reasons for belief in God or grounds for God's existence: our task is the different one of trying to say who this Being is whom Christians worship, and by whose laws and standards, as well as by whose goodness and love, they endeavour daily to live.

There is a second reason, however, for suggesting that it is important to be precise about who God is. It is that there are, you might say, in the air many apparently new-fangled ideas about God, which make it difficult for someone who is trying to find out about God to reach a clear assessment. Indeed, some things are being said about God — for example, that he is dead, or that there is a god above God, or that God is in process of developing towards goodness from a mixture of good and evil — things which, to say the least, are not readily compatible with older ideas of God. Such new ideas have caused many believers a great deal of distress: they fear that such a God is not the God of their faith. Their fears seem in the end to be justified when it is even suggested that it is possible to be a Christian and to be an atheist at the same time. I do not wish to deal with such extravagant notions, but only mention them to show that a stand has to be taken at some point, and the boundaries drawn with some degree of definition, or the faith will one day merge into hallucination, and God himself be confused with the world or humanity. But once the stand has been taken and the boundaries drawn, there are, we shall find, not a few of the less extravagant new ideas which have been helpful to serious enquirers into the content of Christian belief in God.

I want to begin with three of these newer ways of describing God which are proving helpful to people who cannot yet make sense of more traditional accounts. The first is to say that God is *ultimate reality*. Generations come and go. Fashions change. History swings backwards and forwards as empire succeeds empire. The universe itself is supposed to be running down, and the sun cooling. Morality has no abiding stability. Friendships can disappear. But when you run into a reality that is stable, that is unchanging, that is finally and utterly self-consistent; when you come to grips with a reality that you cannot bend to suit your fancy or whim, and which in fact eventually brings you to understand that there is a will that is much more important than yours; then, though you may not be able or willing to put a name to that reality, you have stumbled upon God. Sometimes, you may meet this reality in your own conscience, though you know it to be more than your own conscience, above it, stronger than it, and much more reliable. Sometimes you may come upon this . ultimate reality in your relation to a friend, though you know it to be greater than the friendship and the friend. Sometimes the reality may strike you as what makes sense of all the ups-and-downs of human striving and human history. For some people that is how they see God.

Secondly, it has been said that God is *ultimate concern*. We all have in our lives values to which we devote out allegiance, the things, the ambitions, the persons, we count dearest. These are our concerns; our relation to them determines what we think and do; it fills us with hope, and it controls our existence. But the supreme, the ultimate concern, the value that supports and sustains all of the others, is God. Sometimes, a person will substitute, for that ultimate concern, something or someone that is less than ultimate, and give to it or to him or to her the allegiance, the total surrender, the obedience which is rightly only to be given to God. When that happens, a substitute-god, an idol, is created; and the human life arranged around it becomes disorientated; it gets lost. God is ultimate concern, to whom if we properly orient our lives they will begin to exhibit pattern and purpose, and know something of the contentment that God intended for them.

A third way of speaking of God which has become popular recently is to say that God is the *ground of our being*. This view is often prepared for by denials of such ideas as that God is 'up there' — in the sky, or in outer space, or somewhere like that, or that God is 'out there' — far removed from the grime and the guilt of human existence, or even that God is 'in here', dwelling in our souls and possessing our spirits. In reply to all such apparently false views, it is suggested that our existence rests upon, is founded upon, God. He is not one object among many others in the world nor a person among persons, an equal among equals. He is the condition, the ground, the premise of all that has any kind of being.

I should like to add to these three modern ways of speaking about God, two much older — the one from the *Shorter Catechism* which used to be compulsory knowledge in Scotland from the moment children were able to read, and the other from the Bible itself. The *Shorter Catechism* says in answer to Question 4, What is God? that 'God is a spirit, infinite, eternal and unchangeable, in his being, wisdom, power, holiness, justice, goodness and truth.' That definition of God could occupy us for a very long time, but certain aspects only can be selected. It is far from being a fully Christian definition of God because it makes no mention of Jesus Christ — that reference comes a few questions later in the *Catechism*. But in speaking of God as spirit, it draws attention to a new set of facts: that God is not a material existence that we can find physically in the world about us; that he resembles us in that respect in which we as human beings differ most from the rest of creation, namely, in being spirits who communicate with one another by thought, affection and mutually interacting wills.

The second older way of talking of God comes from the Epistle of St. John, chapter 4, verse 8, which says quite simply 'God is love.' Love is for us nowadays such an ambiguous word that we have to pause for a minute to ask what it really means. We have to reject all the obvious misunderstandings which equate it with lust and self-indulgence, with sentimentality and unprincipled acquiescence in any state of affairs good or bad. After such rejection, we find that there are a host of elements in the valid notion of love — the idea of commitment, the Bible called it 'the covenant' by which God promised Israel that one day he would give to them the saviour of the world; the idea of self-communication, of a God who not only gives his word to his prophets so that they can speak about him, but who actively and continually endeavours to communicate to them his goodness and mercy, in fact, his very self; the idea of involvement, of a God, who does not withdraw from the rough-and-tumble of human life and history but becomes involved in them; and the idea of identification, of a God who becomes *one with his people* in their sorrow, affliction and even their sin. 'God is love' is the shorthand way St. John adopted to sum up all these facts about God.

There, then, you have five different ways of describing God, three of them fairly modern, two of them traditional and very long-established. It is tempting to say that these are five definitions of God, but it is preferable to treat them in either of two other ways. On the one hand, we may follow up a suggestion given to us by the Shorter Catechism when it asked the question, '*What* is God?' and say that these are all different answers to that question, which are incomplete if we do not go on to ask and to answer a further question, '*Who* is God?' It is in answering that question that we come to the fully Christian account of God's being and character. The five accounts of God, in other words, ask us to look for someone who is likely to fulfil this role, to meet the requirements, to hold them all at the same time. On the other hand, we could say that these five accounts of God are markers, or indicators, which draw our attention in a certain direction, and when by the aid of the Christian faith we look in that direction we can see the fullness of God's being, what he is really like, as we say. In the Middle Ages they were very fond of offering markers that indicated where God was, and when he was to be found. They are sometimes called proofs of God's existence, but they were not so. They proved rather, that there are certain markers in the world, which point in the direction of a Being who is a first cause of all that exists, who is the source of all the goodness in the world and who gives it purpose. But it requires the Christian to say that when you have these markers around, God is present. So then I like to think of these five markers as drawing attention to the presence of God. But it is only when we know from the Bible, from the Church, from our own experience of God in Jesus Christ, that we can go on fully to identify and to describe the God so indicated.

How, then, does the Christian finally answer the question, Who is God? If I am to be honest at this point, I dare not refuse to answer this question in what may appear to be a difficult way, but which yet is alone faithful to what has been said about God in the Church for nearly two thousand years. I have to say, in a sentence, that God is Father, Son and Holy Spirit. Without going into the details of the doctrine of the Trinity, which is the technical term for this view of God, we can hold that God is, as it

were, God three times over. He is God the father who also created
the world. The world, including all of the galaxies, the entirety of
humanity, and the universe of sub-atomic entities, both organic
and inorganic, has received its being from a reality beyond itself
and upon whom it is finally dependent. It is not, therefore, the
plaything of irrational forces, or of superhuman or sub-human
demons who might at will destroy it. It is God's world, and in it
God has set man, his creature, made in his own image, to serve
him, and to obey him by using its wealth and resources, its
potentialities and opportunities. Man stands as a steward within
the world, answerable to God for the way in which he uses it or
misuses it — to make destructive bombs, to set up erosion over
continents, to fail to feed nations, to bend men's minds. It is
God's world, and men and women are God's creatures. The word
that is used for this Creator-God is father. It may mean that for
those who have known cruel fathers the term is misleading, but as
Christ used the term, and it was a most intimate form of it that
he did use, it referred to God's care for his children, his
understanding of their difficulties, his patience with their
shortcomings, and his universal love for them. One writer has put
it this way, 'He loves each of us as if there were none other to
love, and all of us with the love that he bears to each of us.' When
we say Father to God, we do not necessarily mean that God is
just a great big man in the sky, some sort of glorified Santa Claus,
and there are some writers to-day who want to dispense with the
notion that God is a person and to say God is personal. The
distinction has always been too subtle for me, but I think I can
almost see what they are trying to say — and it is two-edged.
They want to avoid the big Santa Claus notion, yet at the same
time they know that being personal is the highest reality that we
know, and that to deny that God is personal may be to run the
risk of suggesting that he is less than personal.

But God is also God the Son, the Son whom we know in
history, the figure called Jesus Christ. Here is one who is identical
with God's being, but is also identical with humanity, so that he
has been called the God-man. It is a different if not an impossible
situation to describe, so much so that it has been called 'a
paradox', a kind of contradiction, an impossibility if it had not
really happened. This being Jesus Christ, who was born into the
world, lived in an earthly home as part of a human family,
worked at a man's craft, and in and through all these human
situations, brought home by life and teaching the wonder and the
glory of God's love to all mankind. In all of these situations he

made it plain that God through himself was involved in the plight of man, but the fullest evidence for this fact came when he was crucified for man, when he so identified himself with the depth of human wrongdoing that he bore its guilt and shame in his own body to the death on Calvary. The full triumph of the revelation of God's character and purpose which took place in Jesus Christ emerged when God raised him from that death, so that he is now alive, the King of Kings and the Lord of Lords. The Christian therefore when asked, *Who* is God? might be pardoned for saying quite directly, 'the God and Father of the Lord Jesus', the God of whom Jesus speaks and who speaks to us in Jesus Christ, in his life, death and resurrection. But such answer is just a little too simple, for what Jesus has to say of God, and what we read of Jesus, are both dependent upon the picture which the rest of the Bible, particularly the Old Testament, gives of God, his nature and his purposes.

There is still more to the matter, for the Christian faith speaks of God for a third time — God the Holy Spirit. He is the Spirit, we are told, who opens our minds and hearts so that we, in spite of our obstinacy and blindness of heart, are able to begin to understand what God is, telling us about himself in Jesus Christ. The Spirit, according to another writer, is the way in which God makes sure of us. Left to ourselves, we would so easily go wrong, making our idols substitutes for God, and putting God off with all kinds of fancy excuses. But the Holy Spirit, like a sword, cuts through this tangle and opens a way for us to reach God. The Spirit, too, in a sense attends to the detail of our existence. Life, as we know it, consists of detail, doing this and doing that, getting lost in the niceties of situations and losing sight of the big pattern. We are aware, too, that it is in these niceties that the big decisions come to be made. In this context, God meets us through his Spirit, and nothing is too insignificant for his concern or care. That is the God who is the answer to the question, *Who* is God? The Father who is love created us, the Son who is mercy redeemed us, and the Holy Spirit continually and daily brings that love and mercy home to our hearts and lives.

Let me close, however, with a comment upon the question, Who is God? as a question; and upon how we know the answer to it. There are two kinds of questions which we can ask. Some are factual questions where the information we seek is not going to make a great deal of difference to our lives once we obtain it. I can think of a lot of questions of this sort to which I have had to learn the answers, which were of no earthly use. They did not have any life-or-death significance *for me*. But there are other questions which do radically affect my existence, and they have been called for that reason existential questions. If you are starving to death, such a question would be, Where am I to find my next meal? Or if you are ill, Where can I find a doctor? In both cases the answer is of supreme importance to the person asking it. The question Who is God? is of that same order, for it is a question of the character of ultimate reality. Is it good or evil? Is it friendly or malicious? Does it care or is it indifferent? It is a question, too, about my place in the universe. Has this God got a purpose for me? Does he love me? It is a question, too, about my fellow men. How do I relate to them? How can I show to them something of the love that I have received from God? These are questions of significance for my daily existence and the answers penetrate to the heart of my being.

There is one interesting other fact about these existential questions. It is that they expect a different kind of answer from these other factual questions. It is not a theoretical answer but a practical one, which expresses itself in terms of obedience to the will of God for us and of concern for the broken fragments of humanity, the hungry, the dispossessed, the homeless, and in terms of working, caring and sacrificing, for those who are our brothers in Christ. Indeed, we may find that we shall not be able to answer the question, Who is God? until we have answered the question, Who is my brother?

JOHN MCINTYRE

Where is God?

This is a question that more and more people are asking to-day because our understanding of *space* has been changing so radically. The whole horizon of our human knowledge of the universe has been lifted far above our little earth to take in the vast regions of outer space and indeed what we call the expanding universe. How are we to think of God in relation to all this?

In the first part of this reply I shall try to deal with the more scientific and theological problems, but in the second part I will write more simply and directly about the personal presence of God and what it can mean for each of us.

Normally to ask the question 'Where?' is to ask a question about location in space, i.e. a question about some place in the physical universe where we are concerned with length, breadth, height and depth. This is a question which it would be very unscientific to ask about God, because it does not apply to him at all. The being and nature of God are completely different from anything in the created universe, so that his presence cannot be plotted by reference to the dimensions of the universe in the way in which we can plot the place of anything in space, or even speak of the universe as a whole. God is infinite Spirit and cannot be thought of as 'here' or 'there' or 'somewhere' in any physical sense, or even as 'outside', far less 'inside', space. This way of thinking is so inapplicable to God that Martin Luther once said, 'Even God is not where he is, even if he is everywhere or somewhere.' No 'where' is applicable to God, and yet God is active everywhere and there is nowhere where he is not present. Part of our difficulty here is due to the fact that our ordinary language has become associated with certain notions of space that are not appropriate to God, so that when we use this language to speak about him we can hardly avoid the distorting effect of the spatial images that are embedded in it.

It is very important to remember that God is 'The Father Almighty, Maker of heaven and earth and of all things visible and invisible', as we say in the Creed. He is the creative source of all that exists, beyond himself, for he made the universe out of nothing and upholds it in its being by his infinite power. Even space and time were produced by God along with the creation, and must be thought of as forms of created existence. God himself, in his own being and activity, is not limited or conditioned by space in any way, for as the Creator he is independent of all space and time and is sovereign over them. This means that the relation between God and space is not itself a spatial relation — that is why it is so nonsensical, when we pray to God as 'Our Father who art in heaven', to think of heaven as the place where God is located, or when we speak of the Son of God as 'come down from heaven', to think of that as a journey through space. Instead of thinking of 'where God is' by reference to space, one must rather think of space through reference to the creative and all-embracing activity of God.

That is what the Bible does. It does not talk primitive science or any kind of natural science. It does not offer us a world-picture and then try to fit God into it. It tells us that God cannot be pictured in any way at all, for he is completely beyond anything that we can imagine on the ground of what we see or experience in the material world. God lives and acts and is present in his own incomparable divine way. God is only like God. He cannot be observed or demonstrated in any natural way, and cannot be grasped or netted by our man-made ideas. God is Spirit, and therefore is spiritually present and spiritually known in accordance with his own divine nature. The Old Testament tells us that God makes himself present to men through his 'still small voice', indescribably present, revealing himself to them so that they really know him and are certain of his presence. Yet God does this in such a way that we cannot master him or control his presence, for he comes to us as the Creator and Master of all being, while we may know him only in wonder and worship, by listening to him, loving him and doing his will. Thus instead of thinking that God can be known by fitting him into our understanding of the universe, we must try to understand the universe by treating it as the creation of his love and the theatre of his glory.

It was for this reason that the early Church Fathers, who laid the foundations of Christian theology, rejected the Greek view that space is a kind of receptacle in which things are contained, whether they are pebbles on the seashore or stars in the heavens. Instead of that static container view of space, they developed a dynamic view of space and time. Because space and time arise only in and with the creation they must be thought of as the ways in which events in the universe are related to each other and are connected up in patterns of order and change. Far from thinking of God as contained by anything or of his operations as circumscribed by space and time, they thought of God as infinite and eternal who encompasses all things by his divine power, for not only has he created the universe out of nothing but he orders and holds the entire realm of space and time together in such a way that it is preserved from breaking up in chaos or dropping out of existence altogether into nothing. In this way God gives constancy and structure to the universe throughout all its movement and change, and so makes it the kind of universe we can investigate by science and understand by reason. That is what Einstein called 'the mystery of comprehensibility' in the universe, which never failed to evoke from him wonder and awe, although it could not be explained by natural science. It is because the universe is comprehensible in this wonderful way that we can engage in space travel and explore with our instruments the outermost reaches of created existence in galaxy after galaxy, always relying upon our calculations even to fractions of a second. The universe of space and time is thus created by God as the rational medium in which we human beings may live our lives and communicate with one another in enjoyment of all its marvels, and also as the rational medium through which God reveals himself to us and invites us to enter into communion with him.

In working out their understanding of God and space the Church Fathers took their starting-point from the teaching of the Bible that not even a heaven of heavens could contain God, and that all things in heaven and earth are contained by the power of his creative Word. This helped them to reach a profound understanding of the Incarnation, when the Word or Son of God became man in Jesus Christ, adapting himself to live with us in space and time on earth. They rightly held that to mean that he by whom all things were created and comprehended by assuming a human body made room for himself as one of us in our physical existence, yet without being contained, confined or circumscribed in place as in a vessel. He was wholly present with us in the body and yet wholly present to the entire universe; he occupied a definite place on earth and in history, yet without leaving his position in relation to the creation as a whole, for he became man without ceasing to be God. Because Jesus Christ was both one with God the Father in his divine being, and one with us

men in our creaturely being, he fulfilled the part of a Mediator
even in regard to space-relations between man and God. Mere
human beings are unable to make room for God in their finite
natures, or to endure the Creator in their creaturely beings, but
this gap between man and God is bridged by the Incarnation, for
in Jesus Christ, God has opened his divine being to us and given
us access to himself. Just as God in Jesus Christ entered into our
human space without leaving his divine throne over the universe,
so in Jesus Christ we human beings may enter into the immediate
presence of God Almighty and have communion with him,
without leaving our human place in space and time. In this way
Jesus Christ constitutes the actual centre in space and time where
God meets with man in the spatial context of his earthly life and
man meets with God in the infinite power of his divine Life. It
was in thinking out the meaning of the Incarnation like this,
together with the meaning of the creation, that the early
Christian theologians re-thought the whole idea of space in a
more dynamic way, in terms of the interaction between God and
the world, and in doing so they developed what we now call 'a
relational' view of space and time that made a very important
contribution to the history of physics.

Unfortunately, however, this relational view of space and time
got lost, and the old Greek view was allowed to come back and
dominate our thinking, to the detriment of theology and science
alike. First, in the form in which it was taught by Aristotle, the
container idea of space infiltrated Christian thought from the
twelfth century, and then in the form which it was given by Sir
Isaac Newton, it was built into the fabric of western science for
centuries. It is only in our own day that science has finally
rejected this 'box view of space', as Einstein called it, and is now
developing a relational view rather like that which was taught by
the Early Church. In our own modern scientific thought,
however, space and time are very closely intertwined so that we
often speak about 'space-time'. Today we measure space by the
time that light takes to travel through the universe — at the speed
of 186,282 miles per second, or 5,878,600,000,000 miles a year,
which we call a 'light-year', Hence if we find that the nearest star
in our own Galaxy is 4.3 light years away from us, and the
furthest star in the Milky Way which contains about 100,000
million stars, is 20,000 light years away, and learn that the Milky
Way is only one of billions of galaxies, the size of the universe
that becomes revealed makes our minds reel at the thought of it,
and so also does its age! This is certainly a finite universe but it is

unbounded.

When we think of space and time in this way, from the point of view of natural science, such as physics or astronomy, we think of them as continuous relations within the on-going universe and building the vast unbounded field of connection between the bodies and galaxies that make up the universe, but when we speak of space and time from the point of view of God's creation, they are to be understood as dependent upon God's constant interaction with all that he has made and therefore in relation to his divine freedom and power. Then, far from making us think less of God, all that we learn about space in natural science makes it more wonderful than ever to think of him as the Creator of the universe who sustains the entire realm of space and time from beginning to end. God is in no way limited or boxed in by it, but is completely and freely sovereign over it all. This means also that space is not closed to God but essentially open toward him, for it is constituted and defined not only in accordance with interactions within the universe but in accordance with interaction between God and the universe. Here we have to think not simply in terms of two 'horizontal' dimensions, space and time, but also in terms of a 'vertical' dimension which intersects them and opens them out above and beyond themselves. That 'vertical' dimension is *relation to God* which penetrates through all space and time, for space and time are dependent upon God's infinite power and are ultimately grounded upon his creative relation to the universe.

That point where relation to God penetrates like a vertical dimension into the horizontal dimensions of space and time and opens them out above and beyond themselves is the place that is occupied by human being. Man is the creature who lives on the boundary between the visible and the invisible, the 'earthly' and the 'heavenly'. It is the penetration of the horizontal by the vertical, of the visible by the invisible, that gives man his true place, for it relates his place in space and time to the eternal God in such a way that he is not submerged as a mere thing or a mere creature in the vast ocean of the universe. Without this vertical relation to God man has no authentic place on the earth, no meaning, no purpose, and can only wander about in darkness, but with this vertical relation to God his place on earth is given meaning and purpose for then everything is illuminated from above. Unless the eternal breaks into the temporal and the boundless being of God breaks into man's spatial existence and opens it out toward God, the vertical dimension vanishes out of man's life and becomes quite strange to him — and man loses his place under the sun. That is why the Incarnation is so important for Christians, for it means that God has not left us human beings to be shut up within the dark prison of our own 'flat world', but has opened up for us endless possibilities in Jesus Christ through sharing in the life of God. And it is from that point of view, from the miracle of Christmas, that Christians reach their understanding of space and time and the place of man in it all through relation to God.

Let us now try to answer our question in a more positive way by considering the *presence* of God.

Since God is the self-existent and eternal Creator of all things, he is his own dimension, unlimited and unconditioned by anything other than himself. This means that God's presence is just as unique and incomparable as God himself is. It is quite unlike any other kind of presence and therefore cannot be experienced or recognized in the way in which other presences are. It must be known out of itself and in accordance with its own distinctive nature. Here we touch upon a basic principle in all true science, that we know things truly when we know them strictly in accordance with their distinctive natures. That is why in each field of scientific knowledge we allow the nature of what we investigate to prescribe for us the right way in which it is to be known and also the proper way in which it is to be demonstrated. We cannot know persons in the same way in which we know rocks, for persons are very different from rocks, nor can we prove what we know about persons in the same way as we can prove things in geology. Similarly we cannot know God in the same way in which we investigate the stars; no optical or radar telescope will ever bring God within its reach. To try to 'observe' God in that way would be just as silly as to think of hearing a voice by our nose. We hear a voice by our ear, smell a perfume with our nose, and we learn about the stars through scientific instruments and mathematical calculations. In each area of knowledge the ways and means of knowing must match the nature of what we seek to know. The same applies to our knowledge of God, for it is God's own divine nature that must be allowed to prescribe for us the proper mode of inquiry and the appropriate way in which truth about him is to be demonstrated. Since God is Spirit it is a spiritual mode of knowledge that we must cultivate, while the relevant kind of proof is what St. Paul once called 'the demonstration of the Spirit and of power'.

When we consider the *presence* of God, therefore, we must

treat it as a unique kind of spiritual presence which can be known only in a properly spiritual way. Different things are present in different ways, according to their different natures, this book, a perfume, a sound, a person, a mind, etc. It would be quite nonsensical to determine the presence of a musical sound in the way in which we determine the presence of a book on the table. God's presence cannot be recognized in the same way in which we experience wind or earthquake or fire, for God is not present in the universe like something in nature. His is a different kind of presence altogether. We certainly get nearer the truth when we say that God's presence is a personal presence, but it would be a mistake to think that God is present in the world or to us in just the same way in which we are present in this or that place or present to one another. All human persons are creatures and are limited individuals, whose presence is limited by space and time, for we can only be in one place at a time, and by moving to it from another place and leaving that place behind. God is certainly personal, but he is not a limited individual, nor does he have to move from one place to another in order to be present. God is infinitely more personal than any human being, for he is the creative source of all personal being, just as he is the creative source of the whole realm of space and time. God's presence is not restricted or confined in any way, for his presence is the kind of presence that gives existence to everything else and gives it its own creaturely presence. If God were to withdraw his presence from anything it would just cease to exist, and if he were to withdraw his presence from the universe it would simply vanish into nothingness — yet God's presence does not need the universe in the same way in which you and I need our bodies to be present in this room or to be present to one another. Our presence is dependent presence, dependent on the physical universe and dependent above all on God, but God's presence is utterly independent, for it is self-grounded presence, presence that is creative of other presences, bringing them into being out of nothing, and thus it is an infinitely profounder kind of presence than any other that we can know. That is the way in which God is present throughout the universe, sustaining it and caring for it, but it is of course a presence that transcends, that is, reaches beyond, it altogether. In this sense we may rightly think of God as 'everywhere', provided that we do not think of it in any spatial sense, and remember that it is always personal.

However, when we speak of God's personal presence we mean something much more than the way in which he is creatively present in the universe, just as when we speak of the personal presence of human beings we mean something more than their being in this or that place. Among ourselves we think of someone as personally present when he is present *to us*, when he comes within the sphere where we consciously live and think and act, and enters into reciprocal relations with us, when he comes, so to speak, into our 'personal space' in such a way that we both share our 'personal space' with each other. Similarly when we speak of the personal presence of God we mean that he is present *to us within our own personal space*, encounters us in our own lives where we think and act in relation to one another and the world around us, and establishes reciprocal relations with us there. Indeed this is the purest and most intensely personal experience we have, for God himself is the fountain of our personal being.

It is of course in God alone that we live and move and have our being, but over and above that way in which he is creatively present to us, God adapts his presence to us and makes himself known to us in our individual lives. He comes to each of us in our own personal space, shares in it with us, and makes us share in his divine presence in such a way that, human beings though we are, we may have access to our Creator and communion with him in his divine being.

That is what the Bible means when it says that God *draws near* and *speaks* to us, face to face, as it were. Somehow it is through his Word and by the power of his Spirit that he makes his divine presence penetrate into our human presence, communicating himself to us within our human capacities and enlarging them at the same time. That is the lesson, you remember, that Elijah was taught, when he was told that God was not in the wind, nor in the earthquake, nor in the fire, but in the *still small voice*. That is not the kind of voice that we can hear with our physical ears, but the spiritual Voice of God which he makes us hear in our human spirit. It is through that divine Voice or Word that God creates room in our hearts, or space in our lives, for his divine presence.

This is such a wonderful experience that we cannot understand it at all or how it takes place, for when God establishes this kind of personal polarity with us between his divine presence and our human presence, the divine pole of the relationship reaches out far beyond our creaturely being into the unfathomable mystery of God's own self-existent and eternal being, while the human pole of the relationship which we share with our fellow human beings, instead of being cut short or closed by our creaturely limitations, is made open to the infinity and eternity of God.

Indeed it is only through meeting and knowing God personally in this special presence in which he adapts himself to us in our personal space that we can be lifted up beyond our own limitations to know him in his universal presence to the whole creation. And so, it is only through entering into communion with God and sharing in his special presence to us that we can really know the answer to the question 'Where is God?', for strictly speaking it is not a question about the presence of God for God but a question about the presence of God *to us where we are*. God is always with us, nearer to us than we can say, but his nearness breaks through *to us* when we in our place are open and ready for him.

God is where we are in personal contact with him. But that is just our problem, for we human beings have lost contact with God — the connection between us and God has been broken, so that we are lost and don't know where we are. Have you ever been out on the sea in a fog, when something has gone wrong with your radio, and you have no means of finding out where you are or where your friends are, and are lost? That is our predicament as human beings — we are lost. God is not absent from us but something has gone wrong and we have lost contact with him, and can only wander round in circles, bewildered and aimless. That is why the Bible tells us that we may know God, and enter into his presence, only through *forgiveness* in which the broken connection with God is mended and we are put in touch with him again. It is sin that separates us from God, for sin always destroys communion with him. Think of what happens in our human relations with one another when some wrong is done, how quickly everything can get poisoned by selfishness, pride, enmity, guilt and misunderstanding! And think of what becomes of a friendship or a marriage, a family or a community, without forgiveness or reconciliation. So it is between us and God: something has come in between us and God, and the presence of his light is blotted out, rather like what happens during an eclipse when the moon gets in between us and the sun. How many people there are who seem to suffer from an eclipse of God, so that there is little else in their lives but darkness, emptiness, confusion! Something has got in the way, snapped the connection and blotted out the face of God. Something? It is we ourselves, with our sin and pride and self-importance, who get in our own way, and blot out the light of God's presence from us. Only when we are made open and ready for God, only when we make contact with him again, only when we enter his presence through forgiveness, does everything become clear again. Only then, when the light of God shines into us, and we can see and understand even ourselves, do we know where God is and where we are in his love.

Is all this unscientific nonsense? On the contrary. No forgiveness is needed to establish the proper relation we need to have with a tree if we are to know what it is, but we do need forgiveness and reconciliation and love if we are really to know other persons. So it is with God, for it belongs to the nature of God that we can know him and where he is when we act in accordance with his nature as holy love.

That is what the Christian Gospel is about, for in Jesus Christ God has broken through our estrangement and darkness to reestablish personal relations with him in love. The almighty and eternal God who created the stellar universe, who grasps the entire realm of space and time by the power of his Word, has come near to us, adapting his infinite divine presence to our poor limited human presence, and established permanent connection with us in space and time, by the Incarnation of his love in Jesus Christ. He has done this in such a way as to bring us healing and forgiveness, to reconcile us to himself, and what is more, to adapt our human presence to his divine presence, so that we may enter into living and reciprocal communion with our Creator. Jesus Christ is thus the Bridge to God, the one Mediator between God and man, the one meeting place where man on earth can know God the Father. In Jesus Christ God has made himself present for us, and it is in him that we may draw near to God. And so, if you ask 'Where is God?', 'Where can I find him?', the answer that God himself has provided for us, is simply, *in Jesus*. He is the place where God is known, for it is in and through Jesus that the infinite presence of God breaks through our darkness and lostness and penetrates into our human presence: God with us. He who has learned to know God in the face of Jesus Christ really knows where God is.

T. F. TORRANCE

How can you prove that God exists?

Introduction

The first thing to notice about this question is that it is very different from the question about the way in which any particular person has come to believe in God. People do in fact come to believe in God in a great variety of ways. One person has been brought up from childhood as a practising member of the Christian or the Jewish community and it seems to him to be as natural to be a believer in God as to be a member of the human race; he has never seen any reason to be anything else. Another has been overwhelmingly impressed by the character and behaviour of some believing man or woman whom he has met or about whom he has read, and feels himself obliged to admit that the faith by which such a character and such behaviour are nourished cannot be false. Yet another, at some moment of his life (it may have been in a period of anxiety and perplexity or it may have been at a time of complete serenity), has suddenly been seized by a sense of the presence and reality of God which was as vivid and immediate as his sense of the presence and reality of the material things round about him. And another — though such are comparatively few in number — has grappled tenaciously with all the arguments he could find both for and against the existence of God and has come to the conclusion that the former are valid and the latter invalid, or at least that the former are far stronger than the latter. No two people, in all probability, have ever come to belief in God by precisely identical paths; there are as many ways to belief as there are members of the human race. All that I can hope to do in a brief article is to try to show that such belief, in whatever way it has been acquired, is reasonable and worthy of respect. And, from this point of view, belief in God is in the same camp as most other deeply held convictions of men and women.

One point must be made at the start. Anything like a thorough discussion of the grounds of belief would need far more space than is available here. Anyone who wishes to go into the question seriously must be prepared to expend both time and effort upon it. But, again, in this it does not differ from any other important aspect of human thought. Only an incurable optimist would expect to be given a thorough exposition of radio-astronomy or classical archaeology in four thousand words. If this appears to suggest that belief in God can be acquired only by the leisured and the learned, it must be remembered that we are not discussing here the various ways in which belief can be acquired, but how that belief, once it has been acquired, can stand up to rational investigation. Even if one has neither time or skill for that investigation one's belief is not therefore unreasonable; what is important is that it can stand up to investigation by those who have the time and skill. After all, there is nothing unreasonable in believing that Everest is the highest mountain in the world or that King Charles the First was beheaded; but how many citizens of Britain or the United States would know how to go about proving either of these facts? For those who wish to go more fully into the question of belief in God I have made a list of useful books which will be found at the end of this volume.

A further point of importance is this. Believers not only believe that God exists but they also believe a number of things about God and they differ from one another as to what these things are. In consequence, when they use the word 'God' they may not all be meaning precisely the same things by it. For one man the word 'God' may signify simply the ultimate ground of the universe, and the question whether that ground is personal or impersonal may be of little importance; for another the question may be so important that he would refuse to apply the word 'God' to the ground of the universe unless he was convinced of its personal character. Thus, to these two men the question 'Is there a God?' may have two very different meanings, and if this is not recognized confusion and frustration may arise. Further, as a matter of common honesty, it is essential not to take a minimal definition of the word 'God' in arguing for God's existence and then quietly to slip over into a notion of God that is stored with all the fullness of the Christian revelation. Consider the following dialogue:

A. 'God' means the ultimate ground of the universe.
B. Agreed.
A. The universe must have an ultimate ground.
B. Agreed.
A. Therefore God must exist.
B. Agreed. But what is God like?

    A. Well, he must be loving, wise and all-powerful.
    B. How do you know that?
    A. Well, I wouldn't call him 'God' unless he was.
    B. Shouldn't you have thought of that before?

There is, of course, no harm in using the word 'God' with different meanings in different contexts. When a Christian uses the word he will often mean by it the Holy Trinity of Father, Son and Spirit, who are one divine unity of love. Two things are, however, essential. The first is to be quite clear about the meaning we are giving the word in any particular discussion; the second is to refrain from slipping from one meaning to another in the course of the same argument. If we fail in this we shall constantly confuse two questions that need to be kept distinct: 'Is there a God?' and 'What is God like?' Therefore, when we consider any argument which claims to prove that God exists, we have not only to decide whether the argument is a good one or not; we have also to ask what sort of a being is the God whose existence it claims to prove.

After these preliminaries we can now go on to look at some of the ways in which people have argued for the existence of God.

Ontological Arguments

First, there are the so-called 'ontological' arguments. The most famous of these were devised by the great Archbishop of Canterbury, St. Anselm, in the eleventh century and by the great French philosopher René Descartes in the seventeenth. They all start from the conviction that, whether there is a God or not, the very meaning of the word 'God' is that of a being which depends upon nothing other than itself for its existence and that, therefore, it ought to be possible to find out whether God in fact exists by simply analysing the meaning of the word 'God'. One form of this argument (it is in essence that of Descartes) simply says that 'God' means an absolutely perfect being and that you could not call a being absolutely perfect if it did not exist; absolute perfection includes existence. Anselm defined God as a being than which no greater can be conceived, and argued that to suppose that such a being did not exist was self-contradictory. For, he said, if God, defined in this way, did not exist, we could conceive a precisely similar being which *did* exist and this would obviously be greater. There have down to this day been philosophers who hold that this type of argument is valid; one of these is the distinguished American writer Charles Hartshorne.

Most philosophers, however (and this includes believers in God as well as atheists and agnostics) have felt that this kind of argument is rather like the conjuring trick in which a rabbit is produced from an apparently empty hat; you may not be able to see how the conjuror smuggled it in, but you are pretty sure that he smuggled it in somehow. If God does exist, his existence does not depend on anything other than himself; but we can only make this latter assertion if we already know that he exists. If he does *not* exist, his non-existence needs· no explanation. Nevertheless, this line of thought very clearly brings out one important truth; namely, that the fundamental attribute of God is his self-existence.

Cosmological Arguments

Much more powerful are the arguments which start from the existence of the universe or of any of the things contained in it, and which assert that, *in the last resort*, the only way of accounting for their existence is to say that they are kept in existence by a being whose own existence requires no further explanation. The most famous examples of such 'cosmological' arguments are the 'Five Ways' which were propounded by St. Thomas Aquinas in the thirteenth century; many scholars are not satisfied with the manner in which he propounded them but hold that, in spite of this, the general approach is sound. I must stress the importance of the words *'in the last resort'*, which I have italicized above. There are many questions about the universe and its contents which can be answered without bringing in God; these are the kind of questions which are asked and answered by science. 'Why are metals electropositive? — Because they have more protons in their nucleus than electrons circulating round it'. 'Why are some people haemophiliacs? — Because of a mutated gene-structure in their X-chromosome.' Such questions and answers do not take us outside the realm of finite or 'secondary' causes; something in the world is explained by something else in the world, and the explanation itself gives rise to further questions: for example, what caused the mutation of the gene-structure? There is, however, one question which requires a very different answer; this is the question why anything exists at all. This is not the kind of question that science can answer, and for this very reason people who want to explain everything in terms of science try to make out that it is not a valid question at all. To deny that a question is valid because you cannot answer it is not, however, a very respectable line to take; one is reminded of the Master of an Oxford college to whom was attributed the statement 'What I don't know isn't knowledge'! And if there is one fact that is plain about the universe and everything in it, it is that they do not account for their own existence. Scientific explanations can be extremely illuminating and useful, and we should be very badly off without them. But they only describe the way in which the universe behaves; they never tell us why there is a universe at all. And to anyone whose sense of wondering has not gone numb this is really the most insistent and inescapable question that there is.

In its simplest terms the argument is simply this. There must be some reason why the universe exists, and the universe quite clearly does not provide that reason for itself. Therefore, either the existence of the universe is totally irrational, or else there is a being which accounts for both the universe's existence and its own. In other words, non-self-explanatory being requires self-explanatory being as its ground and cause; but there is non-self-explanatory being (the universe), therefore there is self-explanatory being (God). It is sometimes alleged that this argument fails because it does not answer the question 'What is the ground and cause of God?' The objection is, however, quite unreasonable; for, while it makes perfectly good sense to ask for an explanation of non-self-explanatory being, it does not make sense to ask for an explanation of self-explanatory being.

There are philosophers, chiefly of the school of 'linguistic analysts', who do not accept this kind of argument. Some of them profess to be quite satisfied with the idea of a universe whose existence is unexplained; it is difficult to argue with them, for how can you argue with someone who refuses to ask questions? Others (or often the same ones) assert that the idea of a self-explanatory being means nothing to them; we can go with them as far as to admit that cosmological arguments tell us very little about God, only that he exists and that the universe entirely depends upon him. Our understanding of him can be slightly enlarged if we ask what he must be like if he does give existence to the universe. To give it existence must be an act of will and power, so we are presumably justified in describing him as 'him' and not just as 'it', and it seems also to follow that in giving it existence he shows himself to be good and loving. Nevertheless, what will, power, goodness and love amount to in God remains exceedingly obscure, but this will be less of a problem for those who believe, as Christians do, that God has gone out of his way to reveal himself to the human race.

It should be added at this point that for many people the real function of the cosmological arguments is not simply to *argue* us into admitting that universe must have a self-explanatory and self-sufficient being as its transcendent ground, but to put us into the frame of mind in which we are able to grasp in one act both the impermanence and fragility of finite beings and their total dependence on their creator, 'God and the creature in the cosmological relation', to use a phrase of the Oxford philosopher Austin Farrer.

The Problem of Evil

Any full discussion should take account of the problem of evil. How can the pain and wickedness in the world be reconciled with the existence of a God who is held to be all-loving and all-powerful? I have listed at the end of this volume some books which deal with this problem. Here I can only suggest that in the last resort the real difficulty lies in the limited scope of our finite imaginations. Even an infinitely powerful being could not bring good out of evil such as this, we find ourselves saying, when we contemplate some specially horrible example of human suffering or perversity, such as Hiroshima or Belsen. Perhaps what we ought to be saying is: if God can bring good out of even such evil as this, how much more powerful he must be than we are able to imagine!

Teleological Arguments

In spite of the problem of evil, many thinkers have held that the universe does show signs of a design which can only be accounted for if it is in fact under the ultimate control of a cosmic designer. The cruder forms of this argument are examplified in the eighteenth-century writer who asserted that the ears of a horse are slanted backwards in order that it shall be able to hear more clearly its rider's instructions; they have been parodied in the suggestion that we have been given noses so that we shall have something on which to support our spectacles. They have received damaging blows from the theory of evolution. So far from the environment of living creatures being adapted to their welfare, Darwin and his successors maintained, living creatures have only managed to survive if they have succeeded in adapting themselves to their environment. More recent arguments from design ('teleological' arguments, to use the accepted term) have stressed the fact that the universe as a whole and the process of its evolution have been such as to give rise to intelligent beings. Thus, Archbishop William Temple laid great emphasis upon the fact that the evolutionary process has given rise to minds which, although they have come out of the process, are able to look back upon it and investigate it. 'I am greater than the stars', he once said, 'for I know that they are up there and they do not know that I am down here'; and he saw the emergence of mind as providing evidence that there is a transcendent and creative Mind directing the whole process and manifesting himself to the finite minds within it. This type of argument is impressive, but it needs support from others; for, even if the case is made good that design can be discerned in the universe, it might still be doubted whether the ultimate control was in the hands of a single designer or in a kind of heavenly committee. Indeed, it might be suggested that the existence of evil is due to the members of the committee not being in entire agreement in their planning activity; one may remember the facetious definition of a camel as 'a horse designed by a committee'!

Moral Arguments

A type of argument that is narrower in its scope but for that very reason more direct in its bearing on the individual human being is that which is based on the moral consciousness of man. The sense of moral obligation, of right and wrong, of ought and ought-not, has an absolute character which many feel bound to interpret as witnessing to the existence of a supremely moral (and therefore personal) being as the ground of our existence. This 'moral argument' can take as its starting-point either the sense which we all have at times of an inescapable obligation to act in one way and not in another, or the sense of guilt of which we are equally conscious when we have disregarded that obligation and, to use the old-fashioned phrase, have 'committed sin'. The argument has two stages. In the first it is maintained that the notion of right-and-wrong is of a quite unique nature and cannot be reduced to anything else. Even if many of us take over our moral standards from the society in which we live, moral obligation cannot be simply identified with social conformity, for it always *makes sense* (whether it is true or false in a particular instance) to say that I *ought* to do something of which the neighbours disapprove or *ought not* to do something which they think is harmless or even obligatory. Such sciences as psychology and endocrinology have thrown a great deal of light upon our tendencies to act in particular ways, but we cannot simply explain away moral obligations by blaming everything on our complexes or our glands, for the irreducible sense that 'I ought to do this' or 'I ought not to do that' remains. The irreducible character of moral obligation is as much a datum of our experience as is the existence of the world which our senses perceive.

The second stage of the argument maintains that moral obligation is essentially obligation to a person or persons, and that an unconditional obligation can only be an obligation to a person who transcends the whole realm of finite experience while being its ultimate ground. This is specially impelling in relation to moral failure or 'sin'. We are specially conscious of the irreducible character of right-and-wrong when our sin has obviously been an offence against some person whom we know and love, and whom we know to love us; yet we can have the same sense of guilt when there is no human person whom we have offended. It is the ultimate set-up of the universe that we have violated, and we have violated it in a way that can only be interpreted as offence against a person. 'We cannot feel a sense of sin', it has been said, 'against a cosmic process'; yet we have offended the cosmos — the 'whole set-up' — in a way that is identical with offence against a person. Is it therefore too much to conclude that the ground of the cosmos is in fact a person, who has claims on everything in it, including our own selves, because he is the maker and sustainer of it all?

Conclusion

These, then, are the main lines along which religious thinkers have argued for the existence of God. The scope of each is limited, and, as I emphasised at the beginning, it is important to enquire of each just how much it has proved about the nature of the 'God' at whom it has arrived. And I must repeat that very few people can have arrived at belief in God simply by dispassionately following a formal argument. This does not mean that the arguments are valueless. In spite of their limited character, they have two very important functions. The first is to assure those who believe in God and who practise their religion that their belief and practice are not just matters of habit or social conformity, but have a sound basis in reason. The second is to convince unbelievers that religion is a live option for a thinking person and has a claim to be taken seriously. I have said nothing about arguments for the existence of God from religious experience. Religious experience — which does not just mean experiences of intense emotion with a religious flavour, but means the total experience of religious people in so far as it is consciously related to their belief in God — can indeed have for the person who possesses it an impelling and fulfilling character that makes arguments seem of little force in comparison. But just because of its profoundly personal nature it is very difficult to base arguments upon it. For the person who possesses it no argument will be necessary, while the person who does not possess it will find it difficult to see how any argument can be based upon it. First-hand descriptions of it can, of course, be extremely impressive, but they do not lend themselves to brief summary and classification. All that I have been able to do within the scope of this article has been to give some indication of the main types of argument by which thoughtful believers have tried to give rational foundations for their belief. Readers who wish to go further into the question will find ample material in the books listed on pp. 159—60.

E. L. MASCALL

In view of so much undeserved suffering, how can we say that God is good?

This is a question which is constantly asked, not only by those who reject the possibility of God's existence, but also by many who do believe but are baffled by this seeming contradiction. We are told not only that God is good but also that he loves us. Yet our experience of love satisfies us that any human being would certainly do all he could to prevent suffering afflicting anyone he loves. Human beings are not always able to protect their loved ones from pain. But God, we are told, is all-powerful. Logically, then, he ought to be able to stop all suffering. If he does not do so, surely he cannot be said to love us, or indeed to be 'good' in any sense of the word which appeals to us.

Well first of all, let us look at the reasons for believing — or for being asked to believe — that God *is* good. Perhaps the best way to begin is to point out that we all, believers and non-believers, have this conviction that what we call 'good' is what we expect, what we take for granted as the normal state of affairs. It is not simply that it is more comfortable, more desirable to be well, happy, prosperous and so on. We are convinced that we have a sort of right to those things which will make us well, happy and prosperous. In other words we believe that it is somehow natural that things should go well, unnatural that they should go badly. Thus we talk about a problem of evil; we do not talk about a 'problem of good'. To put it another way: we do not ask why people or things should be good, healthy, pleasant, successful and the like. We start asking questions only when things go wrong.

In other words, we have a sort of innate conviction that the good is there before the evil. Suffering is a departure from the normal. The good is the standard by which we judge everything, not *vice versa*. This attitude of mind is a reflection of the more philosophical grounds on which believers base their faith in the goodness of God.

Perhaps you have sometimes asked yourself the question: Why should there be anything at all? This is simply a larger, more comprehensive form of the question, Why? which we are always asking about all sorts of happenings. If I hear a noise, almost automatically I try to find an explanation. Is it due to a car in the street, a passing aeroplane, a piece of machinery somewhere in the building? Now everything of which we have direct experience is like that. Nothing explains itself; everything points to something other than itself to explain it. So the universe as a whole is not self-explanatory; it points beyond itself to a different *sort* of being which not only accounts for the universe, but also accounts for itself — otherwise there is no *final* explanation of anything, no reason why there should be anything at all.

This is what we call 'God'. But is this God good, or is he, like the universe, a mixture of good and bad? Is he somehow defective? Well, in so far as we can apply our human experience to our understanding and appreciation of God, it seems reasonable to say this. In our experience, defectiveness is due to some outside force working on something which, as far as it goes, is good. If my typewriter begins to go wrong, this is not due to the material of which the typewriter is made, but either to the way in which the material has been put together — so that it does not work properly — or to the fact that it has been in use for a long time, so that friction or some similar force has begun to warp the material. It may be that, in the casting of the metal, some defect was introduced because the mixture was not right, or the temperature-setting was incorrect, or, in general, because of something, some flaw, as we say, which somehow got into the metal. The ultimate stuff — the molecules composing the metal — was all right; but the way in which the molecules were put together was faulty.

When we talk about God, we have to be careful, of course, not to think in terms of some 'stuff' of which he is made. He is, as we have already thought, a different sort of being from the stuff of the universe. We have also thought that since he must be self-explanatory, his way of existing is different from that of anything, including ourselves, of which we have experience. He is totally independent of anything beyond himself. In other words, there can be nothing which could introduce into his essential being the sort of defect which we have just been thinking about.

What is more, since he is, in himself, wholly good, he cannot be responsible for causing what is not good, what is defective, what is 'evil'. To go back for a minute to the man who made my typewriter, it is obvious that the better he is as a craftsman, the better will my typewriter be, especially if he uses the best possible materials. Now, when God creates the world, he brings into existence his own materials, so to say, so that the materials from which the world is made — the basic molecules, the built-in tendencies of these molecules, their patterns of behaviour — must in themselves be good.

Why, then, to come back to our original question, is there all this evil in the world? Why is there so much suffering, especially 'unmerited' suffering? Why are there so many horrors of different kinds, all that the poet means when he talks about 'Nature red in tooth and claw'? Part of the difficulty we have in finding a totally satisfactory answer springs from the fact that the problem is not simply an intellectual one. It is partly an intellectual problem. But it is made much more acute by being an intensely emotional one. The sight of suffering, whether human or animal, evokes a vigorous response from any normally sensitive human being — a response which is felt rather than thought. And it is hard to satisfy an emotional demand with a purely reasoned argument.

But, in so far as the problem is an intellectual one, some sort of answer must be attempted. We begin then by trying to understand what this world of God's making is for. The answer surely is that it is for man's use and enjoyment. It is clear that the whole evolutionary process, which is the story of the world, has in fact resulted in the production of the human species as its highest achievement. It has produced many other species, of course. But the study of man's biological development as well as an appreciation of the range of his skills and the power of his mind justifies us in claiming that everything else in the world points towards and leads up to man. Since, then, the thrust of the process culminates in man, it is difficult to resist the conclusion that this is what the whole thing is for.

Even so, it remains true that other species and other forces have their own purpose and their own nature. When we say that the world exists for man's use and enjoyment, this must not be taken to mean that man is entitled to make any use he likes of the rest of creation. Things are what they are. To pretend otherwise is both stupid and, often, wrong-headed.

This is clear enough at the level of practical action. If I am using a delicate piece of machinery, I must respect it, treat it carefully, not abuse it. A pair of nail-scissors may be damaged irreparably if I try to cut stout cardboard with it. Equally, if I use a pair of secateurs to trim my nails, I shall not do a very good job and I may cut myself badly. These are trivial examples, but they serve to illustrate the way in which, all the time, man is tempted and often succumbs to the temptation to misuse things by not respecting them. At a deeper level, man introduces disorder into the world by failing to recognize the moral laws that should control human conduct. How much misery has been brought about in the course of time by the greed and selfishness, the ambition and megalomania, the sheer cruelty and wanton ruthlessness of men in positions of power.

Take, for example, the history of Europe in the twentieth century. Provoked by what he believed to be the oppressive rule of the Austrian monarchy, a Serbian patriot assassinated the Archduke. This set up a chain-reaction which plunged the countries of the world into a frightful war, in which millions of men were killed, millions more mutilated, destruction on a colossal scale caused and the seeds of future conflicts sown. Without seeking to apportion the blame for what happened, we can nevertheless recognize that all this suffering, much of it 'undeserved', sprang directly from human wickedness of one sort or another. Why should these facts be regarded as having any bearing on the goodness of God?

Omar Khayyam, as we know, sought to fix on God the blame for man's wickedness and therefore for the suffering man has brought about in the quatrain:

> O Thou who man of baser earth didst make
> And who with Eden didst devise the snake,
> For all the sin wherewith the face of Man
> Is blackened, Man's forgiveness give — and take!

But this is a very superficial piece of cynicism. We know perfectly well that we are responsible for what we do. 'The sin with which the face of man is blackened' is man's sin — not God's. Sometimes, when calamity overwhelms us, we ask: Why does God let this happen to me? But, unless we are hopelessly self-deceived we do not ask, Why does God let me do this? — when we perform some shabby or selfish action. What I ought to be asking is, Why do I let myself do it?

Earlier on, we were thinking that part of our responsibility as human beings is to use things in accordance with their nature and function, to respect the qualities that make them what they are. In the same way, God respects our human nature, not least that freedom of choice which is one of the distinguishing marks of men and women. God has given us intelligence to plan and freedom of will to decide in accordance with the knowledge and experience we have acquired. But how often do men recklessly ignore or try to ignore the facts of a situation. We become impatient with the door that refuses to open and we use excessive force in trying to turn the key, with the result that the key gets twisted or broken; we greedily or selfishly exploit our fellow-men or the natural elements around us; we 'play with fire' either literally or metaphorically; we do all sorts of stupid short-sighted, wicked things. Are we to expect that, every time, God will intervene to get us out of the mess we have got ourselves into? No, he· pays us the compliment of treating us like responsible beings, even when we behave irresponsibly; he respects our freedom of choice, even when we make the wrong choice. Do we wish that he had not made us free, or intelligent? Or are we asking that he should give us, so to say, only a one-way freedom — so that we should be capable of making the right choice?

Which brings us to what is really the crux of the matter. When we began our discussion of this question, we suggested that the chief reason why people found that the existence of suffering was an obstacle to belief in God or, at least, a problem for those who do believe, was that it would seem that if God really loved us he would prevent suffering. If he is unwilling to do so, how can he be said to love us? If unable, how can he be said to be all-powerful?

Now clearly, if we believe in the power of God, we also believe that he could prevent suffering. After all, Christ, in his human nature, did relieve suffering almost wherever he went. Why, then, does God not do this all the time? Let us be quite clear what we are asking God to do. We are, in fact, requiring that he should go on working miracles all the time, intervening in our affairs to counteract the effects of our stupidity or wickedness. We are suggesting that God should transform this world of our experience into a sort of magical world, a Looking-Glass world in which effects did not result inevitably from their ordinary causes. We are really asking to be deprived of our manhood, to be put back into a sort of perpetual nursery, where a doting mother would see to it that we did not come to any harm.

But, if we are prevented from coming to any harm, the obverse follows that we shall be prevented from coming to any good either. The time comes in ordinary life, when we have to leave the nursery, to begin to grow up, to learn to take responsibility, to acquire experience, often by trial and error, to become men. So it is in our relationship with God. He has entrusted to us this world of his making, to develop its resources, to learn more and more about it, to put its wealth to profitable use. For this purpose he has given us our own special talents, to be used to the full. We are not puppets manipulated by God; we are agents in our own right. Human prosperity or the reverse, is the outcome of man's decisions and man's actions.

There are, it is true, many events in the world which cause human suffering without, so far as we can see, man's choices being involved. The first of these are, of course, the natural catastrophes — volcanic eruptions which destroy a city like Pompeii, earthquakes and floods which cause immense suffering and loss of life, droughts, bush-fires and other manifestations of blind forces unleashed by Nature. What are we to say of these? In the first place, of course, we need to realize that in themselves, these happenings are no more significantly 'evil' than the rise and fall of the tides, or the movements of the sun and the stars. They are seen to be catastrophes only when they impinge on a human individual or a human community. But the decision to settle in that particular spot — Pompeii, Skopje — was a human decision. The decision may have been for perfectly good reasons. The population of the place at the time of the disaster may themselves not have been parties to the decision. But it would be a very crude and childish notion of God which suggested either that he should have intervened to prevent people from settling there or that, once they had settled there, he should have intervened to divert the flow of lava or resite the earthquake.

But why, we persist in asking, does 'God's world' behave in this violent way? The only possible answer to this is that matter is what it is, possessing its own properties and ways of behaving. Fire and water can be put to benevolent use. We employ them in a score of ways every day. Those very qualities which, domesticated, are helpful and constructive, can also be terrifying and destructive. The sun which warms us and enables the earth to bear its crops can scorch and wither. But it is the same sun. An important part of our education to maturity consists precisely in learning more and more about these natural forces, turning them to our advantage, adapting our ways of living to the particular situation in which we find ourselves. Life is a challenge. Only by facing up to it can we human beings become tough and resolute, ingenious and inventive, self-reliant and in the right sense, self-sufficient.

At the same time, we have to learn those other human qualities of compassion and sensitivity, patience and pity, kindliness and generosity. It seems that, in a wholly 'successful' world, a world without hardship and suffering, man would not develop these qualities to any great extent. *Pathei mathos* said the ancient Greek poet — suffering is an education. This is what all men have come to recognize. It is, we may well believe, one of the reasons why God tolerates suffering in his world.

For we need to remember that suffering is something which can only be tolerated by God. There are those who seem to think that God somehow relishes suffering in his creatures, that he 'sends' sufferings in order that men may repent or be 'detached' from the world and turn their thoughts to heaven and so on. To think or talk like this is to misunderstand both the nature of God and the nature of suffering. God desires, he can desire only the total well-being of his creatures. To 'send' suffering would mean to inflict some kind of evil on his creatures. For suffering of any kind — physical or mental, a toothache or the loss of a dear friend — is an evil and therefore contrary to what God desires, or intends. He permits it; but only as somehow necessitated by the situation arising from the fact of creation. But we are surely right in claiming that he can even permit it only in view of some further good, some more than compensating good, to be achieved by it.

In the Judaeo-Christian tradition, when God created the world he saw that it was good. In the story of the disobedience of Adam is enshrined the profound truth that, whereas God intended man for a life of happiness and comfort, that intention has been frustrated by man's own free choice. This is the deeper meaning of the story of the Fall. Not only man himself, but somehow with him the whole of Creation, is involved in what Newman calls some 'aboriginal calamity'. How, in detail, this is to be explained is a mystery beyond any human computing. But we know enough of the way in which man, by his wickedness, his greed, his ambition, his rapaciousness, his shortsighted selfishness, has wrought havoc not only in his own life and in the lives of his fellow-men, but also upon the face of nature itself, to be able to imagine how, on a cosmic scale, the sorry story of man's refusal to respect the laws of life should be reflected in, if not somehow causally connected with, the ills that beset him. We know that the selfishness of one quarter of the world's population can result in near-starvation amongst so many of the remaining three-quarters; we know that laziness, over-indulgence of our various appetites, the frenzied efforts to acquire more and more wealth, the inability to control one's feelings resulting in explosions of anger can cause bodily disease: it is hardly unreasonable to suggest a deeper connection between man's perennial wickedness and the grave diseases which are the scourge of human existence.

But there is one element in the Christian story which is the final answer to the charge that human suffering is somehow in conflict with the goodness of God. The central truth of the Christian faith is the doctrine of the Incarnation, the conviction that a human being, called Jesus, was the human manifestation of the divine reality itself. This is not the place to argue about the idea; but for the Christian who accepts it in the fullness of its truth, it means two things that are here relevant. It means first of all that God himself became, of his own free choice, involved in humanity, in human experience and therefore in suffering. Man's suffering becomes, mysteriously, an element in God's experience. Therefore, however we are to explain the genesis of suffering, it is, on the Christian view, far from being something incompatible with the love of God. It did not originate with God; but it has been taken up, as it were, into the love of God.

Further, on the Christian view, this very association with God has turned suffering into the very medium of our redemption. Again, this is not the place to expound in full the doctrine of the Atonement. But, whatever theory we adopt to explain it, all Christians are agreed that it is somehow linked with the sufferings of Christ. It was because Christ suffered and died that men are redeemed. In other words, the supreme horror of Christ's agonizing death was also the supreme and final victory over man's self-destruction. Good Friday and Easter Day, Calvary and the Resurrection, are indissolubly linked in the Christian scheme of things. The mystery of suffering is, in one sense, darkened by the mystery of the Atonement; but, at least, it is no longer possible for the Christian to argue that suffering is somehow incompatible with God's goodness.

It is true that this final answer is valid only for the man or woman who does accept the Christian view of life. But, all the Christian mysteries have their analogues in our ordinary life. Suffering, even at the natural level, can be a purifying and inspiring process. It would be fatuous to suggest that this is invariably or necessarily true. But it happens sufficiently often to make it legitimate for us to argue that suffering, an evil thing in itself, can yet be turned to good account. The immense outpouring of compassion and tender care which the sight of human suffering evokes is as great and important a reality as the suffering itself. So too is the courage and patient endurance so often manifested by those in acute pain. Linked, therefore, with the fact of suffering are features which we should never allow ourselves to forget.

Moreover, if our faith in the goodness of God is strong enough we shall see that that very goodness demands that there must be something to offset the horror of suffering, there must be some good at least as great as the evil. Otherwise we are driven to suppose that a loving God allows evil to prevail over good. Though we cannot see the final balance, we can be certain that when it comes to be struck it will manifest more than a mere marginal benefit. All the traditional language and imagery about the final glory to be revealed must be no more than a hopelessly inadequate attempt to describe the final and enduring state of affairs. In a much deeper sense than the words themselves might seem to suggest: *Souffrir passe: avoir souffert ne passe pas.* Suffering has an end; the effects of suffering abide. Or, in the words of St. Paul: 'The sufferings of the present time are not worthy to be compared with the glory that shall be revealed. . . .'

To sum up: the final answer to the problem of human suffering is to be found only in the Christian view of Christ's redemptive activity. Nevertheless, even at the level of ordinary human calculation, though no argument will serve to blunt the emotional impact of the sight of suffering, enough rational considerations can be advanced to show that that suffering cannot be used as an argument against the goodness of God. It is within man's power to reduce the scale of human suffering to a degree that is incalculable. The fact that men do not respond to the challenge is, of course, an argument against their goodness, hardly against the goodness of God.

T. CORBISHLEY

If God is good why does he allow evil things (diseases, disasters, etc.) on the earth?

A few years ago I tried to hatch out a Poplar blue moth from a caterpillar which was just entering the chrysalis stage. I was horrified to see emerging from the encased caterpillar two little reddish creatures which I later identified as the grubs of the ichneumon fly. These wretched things had come from eggs laid in the body of the caterpillar by a parent fly and there they had lived parasitically — eating everything yet instinctively leaving only the caterpillar's vital organs, so that the poor thing would still live and eat until they had done with him. Within an hour of my discovery I was in church saying 'All thy creatures praise thee, O Lord'. Now it may be that there is nothing evil about this — perhaps I was wrong to moralize about an event in nature. What I can say is that I experienced then a revulsion, a disgust, an open gap in my belief, similar to what I feel when hearing of a senseless accident. At the heart and edge of reality as we know it there is horror — from the avalanche crushing to death a crowd of young skiers on the French alps, to the choking of an eight months old baby by its catarrhal phlegm, from the earthquake of Agadir to the creeping paralysis in a girl of eighteen. We have clearly not by a long chalk answered the problem by saying that all evil is caused by man. The very conditions of life include the possibility of non-human 'evil' things happening to us. How then do we speak of 'God the Father Almighty, Maker of heaven and earth'? If we just go on the facts alone as everyone knows them we can and do make many guesses at a solution: we can give up a belief in one of the words of the creed — we can then say God is Good but not almighty, i.e. he is a Father living with his children in a jerry-built, rat-infested house which is the best he could manage, and comforts his family with a helpless pity when they fall foul of the accident-ridden place (but is cancer just an accident?). We could give up our belief in God as the only 'Maker' and say he made only 'all things bright and beautiful' but diphtheria germs and 'all things dark and ugly' were made by an anti-God. We could give up our faith in God, as many do, and say that the whole world is just an accident itself — myself included — and it is therefore useless to look for any sense in it at all. Another series of answers which seem to come from the side of belief includes making God responsible for everything, but saying if we only knew all we would see it was all for our good, or that God does not will things to be so but only permits them to be. Somehow or other, we feel, these look like dodges and not really facing the question. Some people have even denied the question by denying the existence of evil by saying all these horrors are in our mind and if only we could think right we would be able to see them as good. This seems to most of us even more dotty than the absurd world we live in — even allowing for the possibility that a lot we call evil is not really so.

Whatever we say about it we must not make light of the real problem. For most of us we seem to be faced with an outer world which seems brutally unconcerned with the precious loves and lives of human beings. Nature, which on the one hand sustains us, seems to be out of gear with our fragile frail existence and we are not at home in a Father's house which includes in it a chamber of horrors.

This question of evil above all forces us back behind our own attempts at an answer, behind all our guesses and dodges, to look at the heart of the Gospel, to see if we can see what *faith* sees, not faith that believes in spite of the facts but a faith that looks at all the facts, and one fact — the greatest fact for faith — is that there is a place where it is claimed understanding is given and an 'answer' is possible. (I put 'answer' in inverted commas because it is not the answer to a problem — for evil is not a problem as it meets us but a horror insulting our very existence. Our initial reaction is revolt, not doubt or bewilderment.) God has not given us an answer to a problem, but he has set a mystery over against a mystery. By 'mystery' I mean a set-up that we live in or which invites you to live within it which embraces us and of which we are only partly aware. Just as we seem to be forced to live with the mystery of evil we can and are invited to live with the mystery of good. The fact which faith includes with all the others is Jesus Christ. He lived and had to live with the mystery of evil — in our world where senseless things happen — where towers fell on people, fever took their health and life, little girls died, and death came to his friend Lazarus in full life, where sparrows fell to the ground in winter. Christ himself entered fully into the mystery of evil. The first thing that must be said is that he did not 'accept evil' as good. He came to fight it. Sometimes his fight against it took the form of overcoming it — curing it in others — but more mysteriously it took the form of letting it do its worst. The Crucifixion is not only how Christ became the victim of sin but how he faced the enemy, death, in the faith that it would be overcome if he endured it. He was able to surround the mystery of evil with a bigger mystery — the love of God which seems powerless but in fact has the last word in a world of horror and disaster.

When we have seen this we can begin to see something of the mystery of evil in terms of the love of God. We must not speculate too much but we can say that God in his love first created the world and by doing so gave it its freedom and therefore made it at a risk. Both nature and man are 'risky' bits of work and random and chance are built into the order and structure of the set-up. But that's not the full story for the universe is 'becoming' something. The Bible discerns in nature and man the painful birth pangs of a groaning set-up as it waits literally for deliverance when a new thing will be born of the old. At other times it sees the world under the rule of dark forces whose number is up as a new order arrives. Christ bears all this sadness and longing in his own life as he emerges triumphantly as the new creation overcoming this present world by a triumph of love. His Crucifixion is not just an event but a revelation, showing that crucifixion — suffering and struggle to death — is written large through Creation. God suffers with and for the world and by so doing brings us and all things into a new evil-free life. The love that created a free world is the love that brings that Creation through the perils of freedom to the final victory.

In this death and life game of high stakes God has already, as it were, declared what are trumps. They are not clubs (sheer blind force) diamonds (the power of wealth) or even spades (dogged hard work and ingenuity) but hearts. If you don't pay attention when trumps are called you can't follow the score!

The life and death of Christ was either one large demonstration of how evil, sin, and death have their final way with fragile goodness in a huge uncaring universe, or they are by the resurrection of this Christ shown to be the real meaning of the struggle, the fight, the triumph, 'That God by turning all things to their good is cooperating with those who love God', 'That neither death nor life nor things present nor things to come nor any created thing can separate us from the love of God which we have in Christ Jesus' (Romans 8:28, 38, 39). What was overcome by the Cross was all that sets itself against God, all that frustrates his purposes of goodness and life, all that is senseless and meaningless. To move away to any other standing-place from which we might view the crazy happenings is to move off into our puny attempts to make something of it which usually ends in a cynical disclaiming of any solution. Faith sees in this little man, blotted out by darkness but now shining out in his resurrection, the end of all fear of evil. Obviously this is not a solution of a problem for the mind will always go on looking for an answer which 'explains', but here is a conquering of a mystery by a mystery — the mystery of evil and the greater mystery of love.

We can now look again at some of the attempts to believe in God the Father Almighty. 'God is responsible for everything that happens'. Yes, if 'responsible' means 'finally answerable': his final answer is given in Jesus Christ, and on his own terms — the almightiness of love. God's power is not different from his love and there can be no solution to the problem unless the word 'almighty' has been crucified. What does this mean? It means that if Jesus Christ is really the person in whom we see God then all the ideas of God (even those in the Bible) have to be interpreted in the light of what happened to Jesus. The toughest word that usually escapes crucifixion is the word 'Almighty'. It has a long history in the beliefs of the human race who is always inventing a super-superman with an almost James Bond capacity to create and escape disaster. It has taken Christian belief many years to unpick and remake the word 'almighty' and to see the power of the 'weakness of God' in Christ crucified. Here is the revelation of how the power of God works — by its apparent inability to change one iota of the evil situation but in the end to emerge victorious, not by a wave of a wand, but by a loving participation and sharing in what men have to suffer in a universe where so much seems to be against love, compassion, abidingness and pity. Philosophers will laugh or at least smile, the religious minded man will perhaps need a much more forthright statement about the power of God even if it means shouldering him with evils unlimited. The man of faith will see, as he lives and thinks further into the mystery of evil, the greater mystery of love. The Cross is not merely an isolated event but is something always true about God, just as if the log of time has been sawn through on Good Friday to show us the rings of the grain that goes right through the wood from top to bottom. Your heavenly Father knows that sparrows fall to the ground (as they have done and will still do through many a cruel winter) and he has shown his knowledge of the created world of suffering by the loving sensitive involvement with 'the changes and changes of this mortal life'. What God *wills* and brings to pass is a new creation where the former things are passed away and he can say 'Look, I am making all things new'. In other words this order has had it — the order of sin, chance, and death.

Does it help, then, to say that God permits evil but does not will it? But how far can permission and will be so separated? If I permit my son to smoke cigarettes, though I would rather he didn't, I am also willing a permitted situation which takes account of his freedom rather than an enforced discipline which does not. God has likewise freely delivered himself up to a free and autonomous creation which he will only work with, through, and within to a conclusion at the risk of evil. He can do this because this universe is not his final purpose — it was never meant to be all. It is a universe becoming something, in which evil is being overcome, in which the new is present with the old, and good has to fight its way through evil. The pledge has been given, the final word has already been spoken, and power and love are seen to be one clearly and unmistakably in one place alone — Jesus Christ.

We must add that part of the overcoming of evil is a gift of God to man, who is the one being we know capable of gradual cooperation with this work of God through his mind, techniques, and science, and compassion. Man knows now how to avoid some of the evils disasters bring. He will no doubt be able to plot the line of earthquakes and draw the sting of a tornado, produce ever more answers to his fight against disease. But his pride of attainment is always foiled by the mystery of death and the built-in accident factor of his developed society. He can never make himself the final or first word in all this. He is at his best when he sees himself as part of a massive struggle of light with darkness where the 'Light now shines and the darkness does not overcome it' (John 1:4, 5). Men will know their real greatness and real littleness when they see the enormous canvas of the battle for the universe which is God's. He is for us, but only on his own terms, i.e. that he is Love and therefore Power. This he has made known by Jesus Christ. From him the light already shines out and the darkness knows its night is over (1 John 2:8). 'Never give in then, never admit defeat, keep on working away at the Lord's work always knowing that in the Lord you cannot be labouring in vain' (1 Corinthians 15:58).

R. C. WALLS

What meaning has the Bible for us today?

For the best part of two thousand years the contents of the Bible have influenced the life and moulded the thought of the Christian Church. For far longer than that the Jewish Church has regarded most of what is written in the Bible as its sacred Scriptures. Muslims worship the Supreme Being whose sovereignty over the created world is proclaimed there, and they venerate Abraham, Moses and Jesus. In a divided Christendom the Bible is coming more and more to be seen as the way to closer fellowship and understanding between Catholics and Protestants. No book sells more copies, no book deserves more study. Yet there is no doubt that the intelligent reading of the Bible today is hedged with difficulties.

We live in an age of science and we are accustomed to think in terms of an evolutionary process whereby, over a period of millions of years, primitive forms of life gradually developed into more complicated organisms until eventually the animal kingdom emerged as we know it today, with man as the end-product. And yet the Bible appears to claim that the whole process of creation, including all living things on land, in the sea, and in the air, was completed within a week.

Every other day we read in our newspapers of astonishing ventures into outer space, and we know that our little planet is but a speck in an apparently limitless universe, with untold galaxies stretching out to inconceivable distances, and with the possibility that living creatures, of quite a different type from anything we know, exist in other parts of this amazing world. Yet the Bible seems to know nothing of all this. Its world is this earth, and not a great deal of that, with sun, moon and stars provided largely as adjuncts, and principally for man's benefit.

We do not claim to know all that we may yet come to know about the so-called 'laws of nature', but at least we can say that serpents do not talk, axe-heads do not float, men do not get carried up to the sky in fiery chariots nor do they compose psalms while they are inside a whale's belly. Yet the Bible seems to describe these and many more equally unlikely events as if they actually happened.

Clearly then, whatever the Bible may be, it is not a reliable guide to such areas of knowledge as are dealt with by biologists, geographers, astronomers and geologists. For information on these subjects we turn to the relevant text-books and not to the Bible. Since it was written in pre-scientific times by unscientific people, it is as unreasonable to expect it to take account of modern science as to complain that Shakespeare makes no reference in his plays to electricity or television, and shows no awareness of atomic energy. We do not think any less of Shakespeare's plays because of these gaps in his knowledge. No more should it worry us that the Bible has little or nothing to say on scientific matters, which is not more accurately said in modern text-books.

Another difficulty is that although the Bible appears to be a historical account of the fortunes and misfortunes of the Jewish people, continuing into the foundation and first stage of Christianity, it is not history in our modern sense. It does not provide us with a reliable and detailed coverage of the period with which it deals. Important battles are omitted, politically significant reigns are summarily disposed of in a few verses, while minor incidents and personages are dealt with at considerable length. What archaeologists have so far discovered in the way of evidence of the life and times of the ancient Near East, confirms in general the picture that the Bible gives. But if we are looking for a factual record of the history of Israel and the early Church in the manner of Gibbon's *Decline and Fall of the Roman Empire*, or Motley's *Rise of the Dutch Republic*, we shall not find it in the Bible.

Nor should we turn to the Bible if we want to be provided with arguments for the existence of God, or speculations as to the nature of truth, the origin of evil, the possibility of immortality or the relationship between mind and matter. The kind of questions that have exercised philosophy down the ages are not the subject-matter of the Bible, and we shall look in vain there for ready-made answers.

So far we have been concerned with what the Bible is not rather than with what it is. But it is important that we should not be put off reading the Bible by looking to it for the kind of information it does not claim to provide or try to provide. It does not profess to be a guidebook to modern science, ancient history or religious philisophy. It is primarily a book of theology, a book

CARNEGIE LIBRARY
LIVINGSTONE COLLEGE
SALISBURY, N. C. 28144

about the knowledge of God. It is concerned, like science, with the universe but, unlike science, it is not so much concerned with how the universe works as with why there is a universe at all. It deals with history, yet not as a record of kings and battles, but as the area of human experience where God can be seen to be at work. Like philosophy, the Bible is occupied with the meaning and purpose of life, but it does not ask: 'Is there any such meaning or purpose?' On the contrary, it starts off by assuming as self-evident a personal God who has created and sustains the universe, and in whose service all created things find their true fulfilment.

God, the world and ourselves

The Bible, then, is a book about God, the world, and ourselves. It claims to answer far more fundamental questions than those that are dealt with by scientists, archaeologists or historians. It goes to the heart of the mystery that surrounds our existence and tells us why we are here, where we are going, and how to get there. It deals with our life on earth in all its rich variety, its joys and sorrows, its successes and adversities, and it holds out a promise of a richer and fuller life beyond the death of our bodies. It does not claim to solve all problems or compass all knowledge, but it claims to give us the clue to the riddle of life, and to provide signposts pointing in the general direction we should go, but leaving us free to choose our own route to get there.

Much of what the Bible has to say to us is told in the form of stories, but the whole book itself is a story, the story of what God has done, still does, and will yet do, for the world he has created and for the men and women who live in it. It conveys above all the message that God cares for the world, and that because of this, at a certain point in history, he came amongst us in the person of Jesus Christ. From a Christian point of view the Old Testament tells the story of the preparation for the coming of Christ, and the rest of the New Testament, after the gospels, tells of the sequel to that event.

The Old Testament differs from the New Testament in many ways. Not only is it much larger, but there is much greater variety in its contents. The main reason for this is that while the Old Testament is a collection of the religious writings of the Jewish nation, gathered together over a period of a thousand years, the New Testament is the religious writings of a fairly small community, the Christian Church, gathered together mostly during a period of no more than a century.

So while we find in the Old Testament history, poetry, proverbs, folk tales, prophetic oracles, and codes of legal enactments, the New Testament consists mainly of two types of writing, gospels and letters, the gospels being fairly brief accounts of the life and teaching of Jesus, and the letters being writings to young Christian congregations by various of his followers. Yet amid all this variety and diversity the Bible is one book, Old and New Testaments are part of the same story.

The people of God

The thread that runs right through the Bible, and binds together the patriarchs in the book of Genesis with the young churches to whom St. Paul writes in the New Testament, is that it is all the story of the People of God. The Bible tells of the choice by God of a particular community, Israel, which was to be an example to the rest of the world of how life should be lived in harmony with God and with one another. Enlightened by God through their priests and prophets, their psalmists and wisdom scribes, they were themselves to become enlighteners of mankind, charged with the task of communicating the knowledge of God and the nature of his true service to all nations.

Because of the weakness of human nature, Israel failed in its mission. But we are meant to learn through that failure that more than human resources are needed, even with divine guidance, if the world is to become the kind of place God means it to be. So God comes into the human scene directly in the person of his Son, in the mystery of the Incarnation. Born an Israelite, of a Virgin Mother by the power of the Holy Spirit, Jesus of Nazareth begins not only a new chapter in the story of the People of God but inaugurates a new era in the history of mankind, since for the first time a Man was what all men were meant to be. It was his purpose that the vocation of old Israel should be taken over by a new Israel, at first consisting of a handful of Jewish fishermen, but opening its doors to Jews and Gentiles alike as the Israel of God, the Christian Church. Through the power of the Spirit which Christ gave to the Church, men and women who had committed their lives to him in obedience and service, began to find their lives renewed in worship, prayer and sacrament, and went out into the world as missionaries of this good news from God, to offer to others what they themselves had received.

If we are to understand the Bible, therefore, we must begin by seeing it as a whole, as the story of one increasing purpose, as a divine plan from Genesis to Revelation. Its beginning is the intention of God to save us from ourselves, and its end is the renewal of the life of the world. Temple and Church, Jewish Law and Christian Gospel are part of the same story. In so far as we are members of the Christian Church, we are legatees of the faith and practice of the Old Testament, bound in fellowship with Abraham, Moses and the saints of old Israel, as much as with the saints of the New Testament.

The world of the Bible and the world today

Yet there is no doubt that it requires a considerable effort of the imagination to feel that the world of the Bible, Old Testament or New Testament, is the same world as the one we live in. Perhaps it has never been more difficult than in this gadget-minded century, when television, electricity, jet-planes, and technological and electronic developments have revolution-ized, in the West at any rate, a way of life which until recent years had gone on more or less unchanged since biblical times. The outlook and daily concerns of shepherds, farmers, villagers and fishermen are not easy to relate to life in an automated factory or a city skyscraper.

Moreover, even with the most modern translations of the Bible in our hands, we are still faced with a vocabulary and thought-forms which are unfamiliar and often hard to grasp. What does the Bible mean by such words or phrases as covenant, Kingdom of God, Messiah, justification? How do we square with modern medical and psychiatric practice the biblical assumption that desease and insanity are caused by demon-possession, or that the various parts of the human body — heart, liver, kidneys, bowels — are literally the sources of our emotions?

Nevertheless, whatever changes have taken place in our way of life, in our everyday vocabulary and in our scientific understand-ing, the Bible retains its power over men's minds because its basic concern is with things that go deeper than any of these. We want to know how to keep our feet in a world that is in disarray and confusion, by finding a meaning and a purpose in all that goes on. We want to feel that life matters, that we are not like Fabre's caterpillars, crawling round and round in a dish in endless procession until they die. We have immortal longings in us and we want to know if beauty, goodness and truth are merely words. We ask ourselves if it makes any difference what we do from day to day, or whether it will be all the same a hundred years from now.

These are the big questions that men and women have always

asked and they are equally or even more relevant today. And these are the questions with which the Bible is concerned, and to which it gives answers that are as valid in the twentieth century as they were when the Bible was written. The story that the Bible tells was acted out on a tiny stage in a corner of the Near East, in times far removed from our own, but the men and women who played their roles faced the same problems as we do. They shared the tensions of adolescence, middle-age, and declining years. They fell in love and got married, coped with the upbringing of their families, were sometimes struck down by illness or adversity, sometimes exhilarated with success.

Stumbling, falling, picking themselves up, saints and sinners, wise and foolish, rich and poor, strong and weak — this is human nature as we know it today, and this is how it has always been. But the men and women of the Bible saw life in a context that made sense. They were able to confront whatever befell them because they believed in God, believed that they mattered, believed that God had a purpose for them. They saw their lives as members of a community whose mission was reconciliation, the breaking down of barriers of class, race and colour which separated men from men, and the breaking down of political and economic barriers which separated society from God.

And so it is to learn the secret of coping with life, with adversity, suffering and death, and to learn how we can help to make our society healthier and happier for all concerned, that we turn to the Bible. As we have seen, it claims that this is the intention of God, Creator of the universe and Lord of history, and it outlines his plan for achieving this purpose. The working out of this plan, and the realization of this purpose, depend upon the existence of a community, the People of God, consisting of men and women who have been called by God, and who have responded to his summons. They, in their turn, have become this kind of community, dedicated to the service of God, because of certain things that have happened in history.

Poetry, Myth and Legend

It is for this reason that the Bible is not a collection of moral precepts, or a handbook to what constitutes the good life, but a record of the events which brought this community, the Christian Church, into being. Here, however, another difficulty arises. For when we turn to the Bible expecting to find such a factual narrative, we discover that the Bible is never content to record facts without at the same time drawing attention to their significance. What we are given consistently is fact plus interpretation. When, for example, at the beginning of the story of Israel's fortunes, Abraham leaves Mesopotamia and begins the long trek which eventually brings him to Canaan, a secular historian would describe this as a normal tribal migration, common among the nomadic people in that part of the world. The Bible, however, sees Abraham's departure from his homeland as a direct response to a summons from God.

But apart from being more interested in the meaning of events than in prosaic descriptions of the events themselves, omitting those which they consider to have no particular significance in the story of the People of God, and underlining those which have, the biblical writers use poetry, myth and legend, where they think they will serve their purpose better than factual statements. The Creation story in the first chapter of Genesis, for example, is not an attempt to give a scientific account of the origin of the universe and its inhabitants. It is a splendid poem, celebrating the sovereign power of God, who brought into being all that exists, and affirming right at the beginning of the Bible that the created world is not the result of a series of flukes or accidents, or the product of some blind fate, but the work of a purposeful and beneficent Creator.

Most of us would recognize that the power of evil in the world is a hard fact with which we have to reckon. However we explain it, it is more than the sum total of the lapses of ordinary fallible mortals. Manifestations of mob violence in race riots, or the calculated sadism of Nazi concentration camps and gas-chambers, have a demonic character, as have their instigators and organizers. The Bible establishes this fact of experience in the myth of the fallen angels, which, by its very obscurity, suggests, more vividly than any lengthy sociological study, the demonic quality of human depravity and perversion.

The most memorable event in the Old Testament is the escape of the Israelites, under the leadership of Moses, from the threat of extinction in Pharaoh's slave-gangs. It marked the beginning of Israel's life as a nation, and of her distinctive faith and moral code. But in reading the record of the Exodus, we have to sift the probable historical happenings from the mass of legends which have grown up around it and are included in the narrative. Yet these very legends convey, better than the sober pen of a historian, Israel's profound conviction that this was an act of God whereby dramatically he called his people out of darkness into light, out of a living death into the gateway to freedom. So it is with the legends that are told of later figures such as Elijah and Elisha. They do not provide us with material for factual biographies, but like the legends told of the early Christian saints, they reflect the deep impression these men made on their contemporaries, and tell us much about the kind of people they were.

Is the Old Testament reliable?

But the question obviously arises, if the Bible deals in interpretation more than in fact, in theology more than in history, and if its writers were equally ready to use poetry, myths and legends in telling their story, how much of it can we believe? Let us deal with the Old and New Testaments separately, for the answer is different in each case. The earliest narrative writing in the Old Testament probably dates from the tenth century B.C. in the reign of Solomon. It contains stories of the patriarchs dating back to the time of Abraham, about seven centuries earlier. Such stories were in all likelihood preserved at various sanctuaries and handed on by word of mouth to successive generations.

Although archaeologists tell us that the general picture given in the Bible of these early times corresponds to what excavations reveal of the habits and customs of the ancient Near East, we cannot regard the stories of the patriarchs as historical in the modern sense. There is no reason to doubt that Abraham, Isaac and Jacob were historical figures, or that their distinctive differences in personal character have been faithfully preserved. Oriental memories were better trained than our own. Moreover, in an age where there were fewer distractions, and men depended on story-tellers and ballad-singers rather than on the written word, there was a check on the details of a story exercised by the community, which would object, like a small child today who is being told a fairy story, if the narrator departed from the familiar form of the tale.

But when all is said and done, it would be too much to expect that conversations could be handed on accurately for centuries, that incidents in the life of one patriarch could not be mistakenly attributed to another, and that pious tales would not tend to grow in the telling. As we have seen, legends grew up around the Exodus, and if we compare the books of Joshua and Judges, we can see for ourselves that the idealized picture given in Joshua of a whirlwind conquest of Canaan by the Israelites is not borne out by the more sober narrative of Judges. We are on more solid ground when we come to the so-called historical books of Samuel and Kings. But even here we should remember that the Hebrews included these books among the 'Former Prophets', and regarded them principally as illustrative material showing that the teaching of the 'Latter Prophets' — Amos, Hosea, Isaiah and the rest — had been proved to be correct by the actual course of events in Israel's history.

As far as the Old Testament is concerned, modern scholarship would generally agree that the early chapters of Genesis, the first eleven chapters, are not history at all but myths or parables. From chapter twelve to the end of the book of Genesis (Abraham to Joseph), there is more legend than history, while from the Exodus onwards there is more history than legend. Each incident or passage has to be examined and weighed up critically on its own merits, with the aid of the commentaries which are now available in such plenty.

By and large, however, the broad sweep of the story that the Old Testament tells is vouched for not only by the independent evidence of the great prophets, who lived through much of it and who provide a running commentary on the events of their times, but also by what has so far been discovered by archaeologists in Mesopotamia, Egypt and Palestine itself. It should also be added that our obsession, born of our upbringing in an age of science, with the question: 'Did this or that happen precisely as it is described in the Bible?', was not shared by the ancient Hebrews. They were much more concerned to ask: 'What is the point of this story? What is it saying to us?' It would therefore not occur to them to ask whether in fact Jonah was swallowed by a whale, or whether Lot's wife was actually turned into a pillar of salt. In those cases they would look for the lesson that the story was trying to teach.

Is the New Testament reliable?

When we turn to the New Testament, both the problem and the answer are very different. In the first place, it is much more important that we should know where we stand with regard to the life and teaching of Jesus and the growth of the early Church, than that we should know whether Moses had a magic rod or if Elijah was fed by ravens. Unless we can be reasonably certain that what is recorded in the gospels and in the book of Acts did in fact happen more or less as it is described, and is not a mixture of myths and legends, then the Christian faith is built upon sand and the creeds of the Church are meaningless.

We must, however, be sensible about this. There was no

miraculous preservation of the New Testament, guarding it from all possible error, any more than there was in the case of the Old Testament. We cannot say with absolute certainty: 'These are exactly the words that Jesus spoke on such and such an occasion', or: 'This is precisely what happened at such and such a place at such and such a time.' On the face of it we should say that a short, crisp saying of Jesus, such as those contained in the Sermon on the Mount, probably often repeated and carefully memorized by his disciples, is more likely to be accurately preserved than the recollection of a single event, perhaps startling, like the story of the Transfiguration.

We must make allowance for the fallibility of human memories, for occasional misunderstanding, for pious exaggeration. Above all we must remember that in the New Testament, as in the Old, it is the meaning of the events rather than the bare record of what happened that interests the writers most. The authors of the gospels did not set out to write biographies of Jesus, otherwise they would have said much more about his appearance, his boyhood and young manhood, his work as a carpenter in Nazareth. St. Luke, in writing in the book of Acts of the story of the early Church, would have needed far more than twenty-eight short chapters, if he had intended to tell the whole story of these thirty momentous years. The New Testament writers had to select, omit, amend and interpret the material that came into their hands.

Once the gospels were written, they were subject to the same vicissitudes as other ancient writings. Copying manuscripts by hand for circulation gives rise to errors, caused by scribes missing out words or lines, repeating words twice, and so on. From time to time some scribe would correct what he thought was a mistake, or add some comment of his own. By painstaking scholarship over the past century most of these intentional or unintentional errors have been detected and put right, but a margin of doubt always remains.

Despite these qualifications, however, which must be made if we are dealing responsibly with the New Testament, we have every reason to say that we have in the gospels and in the book of Acts all that we need to know about the life and teaching of Jesus, and the earliest stage of the Church which he founded. What we find there is not the product of inventive Christian myth-makers, but reliable evidence which we can trace back to people who actually saw and heard what is now recorded in permanent form.

The Divine Drama

If we turn to the question of how best to read the Bible there is no single answer. Much depends on the individual. Some prefer to follow a course of daily Bible readings with the help of a commentary, or notes in pamphlet form provided by one or other of the Bible-reading societies. Others will make use of a lectionary. Others, again, will find it best to read through a book at a sitting. Fewer, perhaps, will undertake to begin at Genesis and work through to Revelation. There is no golden rule in this matter.

But whatever method we adopt it is essential that we should have at the back of our minds — or preferably in the forefront — a picture of the Bible as a whole, otherwise the particular passage we are reading may be as meaningless as an isolated piece of a jig-saw puzzle. We may think of the whole Bible as a great tapestry, like the Bayeux Tapestry, which tells the story of the acts of God in history. Perhaps even better, since the figures on tapestries can often appear formal and wooden, we may think of it as a historical pageant, with living characters and plenty of action. Best of all would be to think of the Bible as a great drama, with God in the title role and a cast which includes patriarchs and kings, prophets and apostles, but also a large number of ordinary men and women. However, we are not merely spectators of the drama, for we are ourselves included in the cast and the play still goes on.

Try to look on the Bible as this great drama of the acts of God, and think of the first few chapters of Genesis as a prologue to the drama, the picture of men and women as God meant them to be and the picture of us as we are. It is a contemporary picture, because we are all Adam and Eve, and Cain and Abel. We are all the men who try to build the Tower of Babel and make ourselves gods. The prologue is our human situation. Them comes Act I, the rest of the Old Testament. It is the story of how God chose a people to be the means of bringing mankind to its senses and of making the world the kind of place it ought to be. It is a long act, because we have to learn through the experience of other men and women, these characters in the Old Testament, the mistakes we make, and the follies we are guilty of. They have been guilty of them too, and from them we can learn. But above all we have to be shown by their failure that we need more than good advice from prophets and psalmists to bring us to God.

So the drama moves on to Act II in the pages of the gospels. God comes himself into the human scene, comes down to our level to lift us up to his, to give us the power of new life through the Holy Spirit. The rest of the New Testament, Act III, is the sequel. It is the story of how the gospel worked out in practice. Beginning with a handful of men and women, this reformed community of the People of God went out into the world, following the example of Christ, committed to him, and empowered by his Spirit. They went out to turn the world upside down, to reconcile man with man, race with race, and class with class. And Act III still goes on wherever men and women in the name of Christ are trying to carry on Christ's work.

But so often this is difficult and so often we lose heart. That is why the Bible does not leave us wondering how it will all end. It gives us an epilogue in the book of Revelation, which shows us in marvellous imagery and poetry the ultimate end of the purpose of God; the gathering together of all his people in his presence. Since the outcome is in God's hands and not in ours, the final message of the divine drama is to put our trust in him and in his Word, which he has given us for our comfort and our inspiration.

WILLIAM NEIL

Why is the Bible called the Word of God?

The Bible as Word of God

The Bible is almost always read when services of worship take place. Even when the service takes a musical form, the chances are that words from the Bible will be used. As everyone knows, Handel's *Messiah* draws its words from the Bible. At ordinary services it is very usual to introduce the Bible readings with the phrase: 'Hear the Word of God', or: 'Let us read the Word of God.' We may have heard this formula so often that we fail to appreciate how momentous its meaning is. Here is a book — perhaps rather a big book, printed two columns to a page, and the columns chopped up into what are called verses, the English used sometimes rather archaic but often now, as in the New English Bible, brought up to date. This book is opened, someone reads from it, and the reading is solemnly introduced by the preface: What you are listening to (or perhaps not bothering to listen to) is the Word of God. Why 'Word of God'? what is meant?

The Bible has attracted great respect and reverence. For the moment we go back no farther than Reformation times. Then, as has been finely said, 'Greece awoke from the grave with the New Testament in her hand.' This means that about the time of the Renaissance interest in the Greek language was rekindled; and one of the treasures rediscovered was the collection of writings belonging to the New Testament, written originally in Greek. John Knox pays his tribute: 'Then might have been seen the Bible lying almost upon every gentleman's table. . . . Others would glory: O how often have I been in danger for this book . . . thereby did the knowledge of God wondrously increase.' The words of Sir Walter Scott as he lay stricken in a last illness are well known but still bear repetition. He wished his son-in-law Lockhart to read to him; and when asked from what book, he replied: 'Need you ask? there is but one.' It has long been a custom — perhaps not so common now — for people at Church to look up the lessons when they are being read, and to follow them in their own Bibles. In a cathedral I know Bibles lie at the end of every pew for people to take and use in this way. A late Principal of the University of Aberdeen used to have before him not an ordinary Bible, but the Hebrew of the Old Testament and the Greek of the New Testament — perhaps so that he could check up on the exegesis of the preacher!

Of course all this respect accorded to the Bible does not make it the Word of God. Indeed just the other way round: the Bible won this respect because it was held to be the Word of God. Before the Authorised Version appeared in 1611, an earlier version known as the Genevan Bible had been commended by the General Assembly. In 1575 the General Assembly characterised it as 'the common book of the Kirk, a most meet ornament for such a place and a perpetual registrar of the Word of God'. The last words are particularly interesting. They tell us that Bible and Word of God are not one and the same thing: there is some distinction between them, but also a close relation. The Bible is the official record of the Word of God. The Bible itself tells us this. 'Word' and 'Word of God' are phrases that occur in the Bible, and they are not equivalent to the Bible as such. In The Old Testament the phrase 'Word of God' is pretty infrequent. But the equivalent phrase 'the Word of the Lord' occurs very often. When you add to it such phrases as 'the Lord said' and 'thus says the Lord', there is scarcely a book in the Bible where one or more of the phrases do not appear. 'The word of the Lord came to Hosea' (Hos. 1:2) is a simple example. When the Word came to him Hosea recorded what God was saying to him: he made a written record of the Word of God. So too the New Testament makes a distinction between the Bible and the Word. The great opening passage of the Fourth Gospel is all about the Word, about the Logos, to use the Greek expression. 'In the beginning was the Word' . . . 'the Word became flesh' . . . 'What God was, the Word was' (John 1:1, 14 NEB). The Word spoken of here is clearly not the Bible — it is God's Word but it does not coincide with the Scriptures of the Old and New Testaments. The Word as thus used refers to Jesus Christ himself. The Fourth Evangelist is writing what comes to be part of the Bible; and what he writes refers to Jesus Christ. The Fourth Evangelist compiles a written Word of God about him who is essentially God's Word.

Another distinction is apparent in the Bible itself. In Acts 10:36—42 Peter talks about 'the Word which God sent' and declares that this is what God 'commanded us to preach'. This then is not a written Word but a spoken Word. Preaching by which Jesus Christ is made known is also the Word of God. This is a third meaning. Summarizing we can put it thus. Central, essential and primary there is Jesus Christ who is God's Word in the flesh – *the Word of God incarnate*. Then there are the documents we now have gathered within the covers of the Bible and testifying to this Word of God incarnate – this is *the Word of God written*. Besides this there is the unwritten Word of God, for when a man declares the Gospel this too is the Word of God – it is *the Word of God preached*. The hymn is right that begins: 'O Word of God Incarnate' (*Church Hymnary* 198). The phrase used at the beginning of this essay is right: the Bible is the Word of God written. And the expression often used in the prayer with which a sermon concludes is right too: we rightly ask for God's blessing on the 'preaching of his holy Word'.

Meaning of 'the Word of God'

The phrase 'Word of God' has a rather complex meaning. But its basic meaning is essentially simple. Let us suppose that I am alone in the house which is itself rather isolated. It is evening and all is quiet. Then I hear a sound which seems to come from outside the house. What can it be? the branch of a tree brushing the window? a roaming cat dislodging a flowerpot? snow softly falling from the roof into the yard? a neighbour come to visit me? I don't know. The sound as such does not carry any clear meaning. I decide to take steps to resolve the puzzle. I go into the hall and switch on the light at the front door. Then from outside I hear a word spoken. Instantly the situation clarifies. Now I know it is someone, not something: it is a person with whom I am dealing, not a neuter element or force. But what kind of person? – a neighbour and friend? a stranger or an enemy? and is he come to greet me or to rob me? Then more words are uttered. Now all my doubts are swept away. It is the voice of a friend, for no enemy would speak like that. The words used tell me that there is a person outside, that he is well-disposed towards me, that I can bring him in and welcome him. Words do all that – they are the means of communication between one person and another; they bridge the gap between them with knowledge and understanding.

It is like this with the Word of God. Whenever the phrase 'Word of God' is used the meaning is that God is disclosing and declaring himself. He makes it known that he is at hand, that he wishes to have dealings with us, and that he is well-disposed towards us. What could be more revealing and also reassuring than some of the things expressed in his Word? — 'I am come to seek and to save that which was lost' (Luke 19:10); 'these things are written that you may believe' (John 20:31); 'God has made that same Jesus whom you crucified both Lord and Christ' (Acts 2:36).

So men have a listening and waiting role. Like the lonely man in the house waiting for the unexplained sound to identify itself, so men are dependent on God uttering his Word for coming to know him. 'The first and most important thing we know about God is that we know nothing about him except what he himself makes known' — so writes a great theologian (E. Brunner: *Our Faith*). But other people have thought we could discover God for ourselves. Men, they say, have looked at themselves. Like little Jack Horner they have said: 'What a good boy am I!' God is like that but much bigger and better. He is like us but in an 'eminent' manner. Or they have looked above themselves, at the stars in their courses and the cosmic vastness, and have thought of God as that which keeps it all going. God is the first great cause, himself uncaused. Or they have looked around themselves and seen the fickleness of fortune that one day smiles and the day after frowns and strikes. So they have thought of God as moody and unreliable, sometimes well disposed, sometimes hostile or malignant. Or they have looked within themselves and romantically thought that the divine is there — man's reason, or his conscience, or some divine spark possessed by him. Others are vaguer: Something is here, they have said, and there must be something to put it there; and they call that something God 'because they don't know what the devil it is' (F. H. Bradley).

When all this is compared with the Word of God and the Bible, two things stand out clearly. This idea of God comes as the conclusion of an argument. It is by search or research on our part that God comes to be known. But is this a true account? When we search and research we push bits of the world about, manipulating them, interrogating them, forcing them to answer our questions and disclose their secrets to us. But clearly we cannot treat God in this way. The Bible puts it the other way round — it is God who does the searching: 'O Lord, thou hast searched me and known me' (Ps. 139:1). The message of the Bible is that God goes out of his way to seek us out.

Further men have thought and dreamed and imagined great and fine things about God; and when stuck for words they have simply said what God is not — he is in-finite, in-effable, im-passible, and so on. But this is not the way of the Bible. Even when it uses negative words like these, it fills the gaps with positive meaning. The Word tells us to say to God: 'Abba, Father'; the Word tells us that God is almighty in the sense that he can come to men as a child born in a stable; the Word tells us that God so loved the world that he gave. These things and others like them are far beyond the reach of the wildest dreams or beliefs that men can of themselves have. They have to have happened to be believed. Because Jesus is what he is as attested in the written Word and proclaimed in the preached Word based on the written Word — for this reason we dare to think of God as the God and Father of Jesus Christ and as therefore not different from what we see in Jesus Christ.

So the Word of God is identical with revelation. God reveals or discloses himself to us in the Word with which he addresses us. He speaks his Word not aimlessly but with a purpose. The Bible calls this a purpose of salvation. In the language of today we may say that the purpose is to enable man to know and reach and be his true self. The Word once spoken echoes and re-echoes with a great variety of tones and reverberations. There is law to give us the guidelines of true life. There is judgment to indicate the ways that simply won't work. There is comfort and encouragement for those vexed with sorrow or trial; challenge for those too easily settling for less than the best; and always glimpses of immense depths and infinite heights. The Word of God opens up to us a strange new world (Karl Barth: *The Word of Man and the Word of God*). Things fall into a perspective more like God's. Our human standards are subjected to revaluation. Meaning and pattern is given to the jigsaw of human existence. But, however strange the world to which the Word of God calls us, we may be sure of two things at least. However mysterious God is and remains, there is nothing in him that is not Christlike; and in consequence, he shows us the way to life that is true and full.

Is the Word of God to be found in the Bible alone?

This is an important question. The Bible is the Word of God, and God speaks to us in it. But besides the Bible there is an immense literature that also talks to us about God. Recently we have become more acutely aware of this. In schools there is a lively interest in what the books of other religions say about God. How do the books of the Bible compare with these? The Church from earliest times had to provide some answer to this kind of question. Today we have a Bible containing 39 Old Testament books and 27 New Testament books. But there is also a fringe of about 15 books called the Apocrypha of the Old Testament, and described by most Churches as useful but not normative. The existence of these Apocrypha books reminds us that the Church had to give prolonged consideration to many other writings that competed for inclusion in the Bible. In the case of the Old Testament, Jerome (about A.D. 400) adopted the answer already given by Judaism. Of the possible rival claimants for inclusion in the Old Testament they accepted the books as we now have them, and they put the Apocrypha books in a kind of appendix. This early practice was endorsed by the Churches of the Reformation. But no such ready-made solution was available in the case of the New Testament. The Church had to make up its own mind. One or two of the books now in our New Testament had difficulty in making good their claim for acceptance. St. Paul wrote four letters to Corinth; but of these only the second and the fourth appear in our New Testament. The Epistle of James was not universally accepted till after the end of the second century; and much later Luther called it a 'right strawy epistle'. On the other hand, some books not eventually included were serious claimants. A work called *The Shepherd of Hermas* was quoted on the same level as Genesis and Hebrews by Athanasius; and a second-century writing called *The Teaching of the Twelve* was regarded as Holy Scripture by Clement of Alexandria and others.

In this situation a nice judgment was needed. On the whole the Church was guided by two principles as it gradually came to authorize the books we now have in the New Testament. The first principle was the extent to which a writing was accepted and used by the Church. The second principle was more objective: was the work originally written by an Apostle or an apostolic man? In fact the Church when it was making up its mind did not possess the accuracy of later biblical study, and some of the judgments it passed are at least questionable. But on the whole the instincts that guided it were right. The works finally selected for inclusion in the New Testament (now taking its place on the same level of respect and reverence as the Old Testament) are at least 'apostolic' in character; they are not all written by 'the twelve'; but they are the work of eyewitnesses or (as in the case of St. Paul) those immediately succeeding them. The authors testify to the incarnation itself or to the age of the bestowal of the Spirit that immediately followed.

When the Church formed what is called the canon of Scripture, that is, the list of books authorized for reading in the

Church, it put a ring round those that in its judgment constituted the first and original testimony to the events of the incarnation and the bestowal of the Spirit, that is, to the whole sequence of the events of Jesus Christ incarnate, crucified, risen and regnant. Nothing is so important as these events; and, since God speaks his Word to mankind through them, nothing in secondary importance is equal to this first testimony to them. Two things follow from this. The Church is obliged to declare these saving events, faithfully adhering to the primary record of them. And too the Church abjures any claim to put on the same level as this primary record anything it may subsequently say by way of repetition or development. There is a difference between what God says to the Church and what the Church says to itself. The Bible is 'privileged' witness. In forming a canon of Scripture the Church has recognized this fact. No wonder then that it calls the Bible the Word of God.

The continuing witness — two other questions

Since the books of the Bible were completed, Christians have kept on writing about Jesus Christ and the Christian religion. Some of these books are technical and interest chiefly theologians. But others have made an astonishingly wide appeal to Christian people. What place is to be allotted to St. Augustine's *Confessions*, St. Thomas a Kempis's *Imitation of Christ*, Bunyan's *Pilgrim's Progress*, Henry Scougal's *Life of God in the Soul of Man*? Some people find such works easier to read and more inspiring than parts of the Bible. Are they the Word of God or not? One thing to remember here is that none of the authors of these works ever dreamt of putting their work on the level of the Bible. Writings subsequent to the primary witness of Scripture cannot be elevated to this place for it is already occupied and there is room for no others. Later writers simply reiterate, and know that they simply reiterate, in their own way the imperishable Gospel definitively recorded in the biblical books. As such they have a limited and also a special importance: limited, because they have nothing new to say; and special because the same things as were earlier and definitively said they now say again to a particular audience in particular circumstances. Can God speak through them? Of course he can, for he is free to make any time or place or means an occasion to address men. But the Bible *is* the Word of God, and this description cannot be simply applied to the other writings that succeed it.

What then about the 'sacred writings' of other religions? what about the Koran of Muslims, the Bhagavadgita of Hindus, the Suttas of Buddhism? The question is not new. The Church in early days had to make up its mind how to regard the philosophical and religious writings of the world of its own day, and especially of Greece, e.g. Plato. Some theologians at that time advised the Church to have nothing to do with these pagan writings; others thought that they did at least provide a preparation on an elementary level for what was definitively said in the Gospel of Jesus Christ. But all were agreed that at most the writings did not really carry those who studied them to the God and Father of our Lord Jesus Christ. We might do worse than learn from this precedent. Nowhere in the writings of other religions is there to be found the idea of a God who puts himself at risk in the world so as to 'become man', who gives his 'life a ransom' for mankind, who is 'in Christ reconciling' the world. If then there is a Word of God in these writings it is not *the* Word of God. God may indeed speak in them to keep alive in men's minds the recollection of himself. The Bible is different: it not only testifies that the most sanguine guesses of mankind are far exceeded, but that the fulness of God has taken real human form in Jesus Christ, the Word of God who was born and crucified under Pontius Pilate, and who by the power of God is raised and glorified.

J. K. S. REID

Is the Bible true? Can you prove it?

This looks like a straightforward question, but it cannot be answered with a simple Yes or No. People who ask it probably believe that either everything in the Bible must be absolutely true or else nothing that it says can be worth hearing: it must be a fairy tale from beginning to end. This notion is entirely mistaken.

What does it mean to ask 'Is the Bible true?' If it means, 'Is every statement contained in the covers of the Bible factually correct?', then, certainly, a short answer can be given: it is 'No'. Many statements of fact in the Bible are incorrect. This can be demonstrated in various ways. There are statements in one part of the Bible that are contradicted in another, and both cannot be true. There are other statements which can be checked against unimpeachable evidence from outside the Bible and shown to be mistaken, such as the statement in Daniel that Darius the Mede took the kingdom from Belshazzar king of the Chaldaeans.

Most people, however, who ask this question are not much concerned with detailed facts of ancient history. If they are, it is because they think that when Christians speak of the Bible as God's Word this implies that unlike any other book in the world it is guaranteed to be free of all errors. Then if it turns out after all that there are errors in it they suppose that it has been discredited and that the Christian belief that in it we can hear the Word of God must be false. But this is not so. What is false is the notion that infallibility is to be found anywhere in this world, and the idea that God cannot address his Word to men through the medium of fallible human minds and sometimes erroneous human writings. What those who ask 'Is the Bible true?' really want to know is not whether all the detailed information in it about ancient history is true but whether its main message is true: whether it speaks truly about the way God deals with man and the way man should respond to God, whether it tells the truth about our human condition, and, above all, whether we can rely on what it tells us about God's dealings with man in Jesus Christ. This is a much more important question, and a much more complex one.

We must first ask what we mean by 'the Bible'. Of course 'the Bible' means to us first of all a single volume printed in English. But the Bible is not really one book. It is a great collection of books of many different kinds. None of the authors of these books thought that he was writing part of 'the Bible'. It was not until long after they were written that they were collected together and marked off from all other literature as 'scripture'. The first collection to be made was of the Hebrew 'scriptures' which Christians call the 'Old Testament'. This was the Bible of Jesus and the early Christians. Then, later, it was not until a long time after the Greek books which we call the 'New Testament' had been written that they too were collected together and placed alongside the Hebrew scriptures to make up our 'Bible' with its two Testaments. So when we think of the Bible we should visualize it not as a volume but as a library of books each with its own title and author.

These books were written at various times over a very long period of history. More than a thousand years separate the earliest of these writings from the latest; and, as we should expect in a collection ranging over so vast a stretch of time, it includes examples of many very different types of literature. Many of the books are historical, telling the story of the people of Israel. Others are books of poetry, such as the Psalms. The books of the Prophets are a mixture of poetry and prose; they contain what we should probably call sermons, political oratory, personal meditation, the wrestling of great minds with the theme of God's dealings with men, his judgment and his mercy. Other books contain moral and practical maxims for ordinary life: the wise sayings so highly treasured in the ancient East. The book of Job is a drama with a prologue, dialogue and epilogue. There are simple stories, myths or fictional tales, with an inner meaning that is not always immediately apparent at first sight to the modern reader. There are visionary, dream-like, attempts to picture the 'end' of the unfolding story of human existence and God's relations with his world: the final vindication of his people against their enemies, and of his justice against the powers of evil. At the other extreme, as it were, there are personal letters like those of the missionary, Paul, some addressed to congregations which he had converted, such as the churches of Corinth and Galatia, or which he intended to visit, like the church at Rome, some to individuals, like the delightful note which he sent to his friend Philemon asking him to take back and forgive his runaway slave. Most important of all, there are the four Gospels, the books which tell us about the words and deeds of Jesus as these were remembered in the first Christian congregations, and which interpret those memories in the light of faith in Jesus as the risen, present, and active Lord. These four books are unique. They cannot be classified in our ordinary categories of literature, for they are neither biographies, nor anecdotes, nor missionary sermons, nor defences of Christian faith against opponents, nor straight history, though they contain elements of all these types.

Now, when we ask of all this mass of literature 'Is it true?', it is clear at once that the question cannot be given a simple answer. We are talking about very different kinds of books, and therefore about different ways of judging their truth. To each kind of literature there is its own appropriate criterion of truth, and it is very important not to create confusion by applying these criteria wrongly. What, for instance, do we mean when we ask whether a great drama is 'true'? Not, surely, whether or not the plot tells us about events that actually happened once upon a time; for, if so, we should have to say that nearly all the great tragedies are 'untrue'. It is highly improbable that 'King Lear' or 'Hamlet' is 'true' in this very limited and pedestrian sense; and only the dimmest of dim-wits would think this fact important. The 'truth' of a tragedy is not to be judged by the criterion of historical evidence, but by the extent to which it reveals to us the truth about our human situation and our human experience. It speaks the truth to us, if it is a 'true' work of art, about our own predicament. In the deepest sense, it 'rings true'. Whether or not there ever was an actual king called Lear is quite beside the point.

Very similar criteria of truth have to be applied to fable, myth and parable. The stories of the Good Samaritan and the Prodigal Son speak truth to us about ourselves, our relations with other people, and God's dealings with us. It makes no difference to their truth that Jesus, as a good story-teller, invented these tales. So, too, the story of Adam and Eve in the garden speaks the truth to us — a painful and shaming truth — about the proper place and duty of man in God's world, put into the world to manage and control it under God's orders; about man's fatal tendency to rebel against the Creator, his selfish, grasping, desire to exploit the world for his own advantage, the mess he makes of God's world, and how, when he tries to play God and put himself in the centre of the world-picture, his world goes bad on him and he finds that he has exchanged the garden of God for his own desert. If we ask, 'Did God make a couple called Adam and Eve? Did a snake really talk to Eve?', and so on, the answer is 'No'. In that sense, when the criteria appropriate to history are applied to this story, it is not true. But it was never meant to be understood as true by the criteria of history; for the name 'Adam' is simply the Hebrew for 'Man', or as we should say 'Everyman'. It is a story about ourselves, and anyone who has thought at all deeply about our responsibility for the world we have been put into, about our disastrous failure to carry out our responsibility, and the catastrophic consequences of human greed and selfishness when man yields to temptation and disobeys his Maker, knows only too well that the story is absolutely true; and he can prove that it is true from the evidence of his own eyes and his own conscience.

The book of Jonah, again, is a book which is 'untrue' in the sense that it describes fictitious events which did not happen as they are told. It is an allegory: a tale with a deeper meaning. On the surface it appears to be a strange kind of adventure story in which a ship's crew in a terrifying storm throw their passenger overboard; he is swallowed by a great fish and afterwards regurgitated. What the author, however, is trying to do is to show us, in a bizarre and memorable parable, a picture of Israel's call by God to go and evangelize her enemies instead of hoping that God will destroy them; of Israel's reluctance to obey, and how she tried to escape her duty; and, how, after being swallowed up, as it were, by her captivity in a foreign land, and after being brought back to her own country, she must now face the missionary task which God has inescapably laid upon her. So speculations about the size of a whale's gullet are as pointless in assessing the truth of the book of Jonah as the old arguments about Cain's wife are in relation to the true myth of 'Everyman' and his wife. In his book *Animal Farm* George Orwell conveyed a terribly true picture of the story of Russian Communism; no reader who was not extremely stupid would dismiss his parable as untrue because animals do not actually talk and organize themselves.

Each type of book in the collection, poetry, drama, myth, parable, history and the rest, thus has its own proper criterion of truth; and the question we have to ask about each of them is first of all, 'What does this book intend to say to us?', 'Why was it written?', and then, 'Does what it says to us "ring true"?', 'Does it chime in with our own experience?', 'Does it throw light on ourselves and our human situation?', 'Does it disclose fresh truth about our lives as individuals and as members of society?', 'Does it open up new possibilities for living?', 'Does it confront us with a claim, a demand upon us that speaks authoritatively to our minds and our moral consciousness and is absolute and ultimate?', 'Does it also assure us of an ultimate and sovereign graciousness, love and mercy which reach out to us from beyond ourselves and touch us?', 'Does it, in fact, speak the word of God to us?'. Not every book, nor every part of any book, in the collection will do this; but the experience of countless readers and listeners down the ages has been that within these books as nowhere else it is possible for those who are willing to apply their intelligence with patience to find the word of God.

Yet the literature of the Bible includes a great deal of historical narrative. In the Old Testament there are many volumes of history, telling the story of the Israelite people. In the New Testament the Gospels and the Acts of the Apostles describe events in the life of Jesus, his death and resurrection, and the bringing of good news about him by his followers to all parts of the world, thus bringing a reconstituted Israel into being, the Christian Church. What people want to know is how far this long history can be relied upon as true.

No simple answer can be given. There is no direct means of checking the truth of most of this history against other records. Some of it belongs to an extremely remote antiquity. It is concerned mainly with the small country of Palestine, a relatively insignificant part of the ancient world both politically and economically. So we cannot expect to find 'secular' historians paying much attention to the events recorded in the Bible. For instance, from the standpoint of the imperial government in Rome the Crucifixion was just one of many executions of nationalist agitators in a far-off province. In fact, it *is* recorded by Roman historians, but only because the puzzling phenomenon of the rapid growth of the Christian movement on their own doorsteps compelled them to say something about how this movement had started. 'Secular' histories fill in the background of the biblical stories for us, but for the most part they neither confirm them nor discredit them.

Archaeology has certainly contributed enormously to biblical studies. We must not, however, jump to hasty conclusions about this. Archaeology has not disproved the biblical narratives. On the other hand, it has not directly proved that 'the Bible is true' in any major respect. A few of its discoveries do bear directly upon things mentioned in the Bible. The famous Siloam inscription is a contemporary record of the water works constructed by Hezekiah at Jerusalem, mentioned in 2 Kings 20:20. Another inscription, at Caesarea, bears the name of Pontius Pilate the Governor of Judaea. There are other striking examples. But these are not very important for our purpose. They might serve the limited and negative purpose of ruling out the possibility that *everything* in the historical books of the Bible is fictitious; but no sane person would ever suppose that it was.

What archaeology can do, and has done most successfully, is to illuminate the stage on which the drama of biblical history was played. It has shown us the kind of society in which Abraham must have lived if what Genesis says about him is true. It has not proved that Abraham did live or that he did not. It can tell us what life in Egypt was like in the time of Moses: but nothing about Moses himself. It can show us the sites and remains of places and buildings mentioned in the New Testament. One particular discovery has enabled us to read the New Testament with fresh insight into its background of life and thought. This is the finding of the library of the strange and enigmatic community at Qûmran: the 'Dead Sea Scrolls'. They show that Judaism in the time of Jesus was more varied and less monolithic than had been supposed, and that there were sectarian Jews whose thinking moved in some respects along parallel lines to that of the earliest Christians. But we must not exaggerate the relevance of these documents to the study of the New Testament. The differences between the Qûmran group and the Christians are much greater than their similarities.

In trying, then, to assess the value of the biblical writings as plain history we have to analyse them critically, like any other books by ancient historians who wrote long before modern standards of exactitude and historical judgement were evolved. The writers used many sources of information, both written and oral. Some of these were reliable, others garbled or tendentious. Sometimes they employed these sources percipiently, sometimes they misunderstood them or altered them. Consequently, their books contain many errors. On the other hand, impartial critical investigation by capable scholars tends to show that the general overall picture of Israel's history in the Old Testament is substantially reliable. This is all we ought to expect, for there is no reason to believe that these writers were somehow guaranteed against the possibility of error.

But to leave the question there would be to say very little. These authors did not set out merely to write a chronicle of things that had happened, and if this were all that they achieved no one today except a specialist in the ancient history of the

Middle East would bother to read their books. On the contrary, the biblical writers are not just chroniclers of the events; they are interpreters of their significance. When their writings were collected together in the Old Testament they were not labelled 'history'. Most of them were included in the section called 'The Prophets'. Now, a prophet is a person who has the spiritual and intellectual insight and sensitivity to hear God's word inwardly addressing him, and to interpret what is going on in the world around him in terms of God's purposes for men, their disobedience, and his judgment and forgiveness. This is what these historical writers were doing when they looked back on the traditions of their nation's past. They discerned God's calling, God's judgment, God's faithful love, God's providential care. In and through the achievements and failures of men and empires they preceived God revealing himself in action, disclosing himself progressively as the God who had called this people into existence and had promised them, 'I will be their God and they shall be my people.' Although their books are so different from each other, this great theme runs through them all and gives them unity; for the promise, 'I will be their God and they shall be my people' is God's covenant with Israel. This is the 'Old Covenant', or as it has been rather misleadingly translated, 'The Old Testament'.

It is called 'Old' because God's promise did not attain its fulfilment in the pre-Christian history of Israel. The fulfilment comes with the life and work of Jesus, God's word made flesh: the embodiment in a human life of God's faithful love. In Jesus truth is to be found, for, as Christians believe, he *is* the truth. Yet we possess no biography of Jesus. The Gospels do not give the story of his life, nor were they written, in all probability, by people who knew him in the flesh. Mark and Luke were not among the original disciples, and the Gospels traditionally said to be 'according to' Matthew and John were probably not written by those two apostles.

The word 'Gospel' means 'good news', and these books were written to tell good news about Jesus as Lord and Saviour. They proclaim their message in the form of sketch pictures of the saving and healing work of Jesus and samples of his teaching; and, more especially, in pictures of his death and resurrection. I say 'pictures' because each Gospel is like a portrait. A skilful portrait is not like a photograph. The artist selects; he adds and omits; he highlights some aspects of his subject and tones down others; his portrait may be impressionistic. Superficially it is not so accurate as a photograph. But a portrait, if it is a good interpretation, reveals the inner character of the subject in a way impossible for a photograph. This is just because it is an *interpretation*. The Gospel writers worked upon the memories of Jesus handed down in the early Christian communities. They selected from these in the manner of a skilled artist, presenting us with four distinct portraits of Jesus, each seen, as it were, from a different angle. They were interpreters of the traditions that they had heard. And they interpreted the memories of Jesus in the brilliant light of their Easter faith. Before his death Jesus had seemed to many people to be a great prophet, teacher and healer. Now he was much more besides; and it was men who believed in him as the living Lord, invisibly present with his people till the end of time, who looked back upon the memories of his deeds and words and saw them in a new perspective. Thus the Gospels give us, not raw facts about Jesus, but interpretations of him: portraits and not photographs.

Question marks have to be put against individual deeds and sayings of Jesus as reported in the Gospels. Nevertheless, the overall picture which they jointly present, reinforced by what Paul and others say or hint at in their letters, is extraordinarily consistent. It does most certainly 'ring true'. It shows us a startlingly original mind, one whose ideas about God and man were often in striking contrast with those of his contemporaries. The Jesus disclosed in the Gospels is an overwhelmingly convincing person. There is every reason to believe that their presentation of his character is substantially true; and, if this is so, to believe also that the ancient faith of Israel which he held himself and which he derived from his Bible, the 'Old Testament', is substantially true too.

Biblical scholars can advance good reasons for trusting the general credibility of these books. But the proof does not in the end lie with them. In the last resort every reader has to ask himself whether the interpretation put by these writers upon the historical events that culminated in the life and death of Jesus is the right one. Did these men have the insight to understand the real significance of what had happened? Christians believe that they had; and it is this quality of insight, enabling them to discern the truth about God and man, which we are talking about when we say that they were 'inspired'. You cannot prove that they were right, or demonstrate their inspiration, by reference to any external criterion. They must be allowed to speak for themselves, and Christians down the ages have found in experience that to follow out the implications of their interpretation of God and man makes sense of life. The truth of what they are saying can in the end be tested only by committing oneself to living by it.

GEOFFREY LAMPE

Miracles and visions

In the Bible there are many things like miracles and visions which we have to believe in, and yet which we have no experience of in our own lives — in what ways or in what incidents has God interfered with the laws of science in the twentieth century? — This is the full wording of the question referred to in the heading: how is it to be answered?

It is perfectly true that the New Testament is full of miracles: there is hardly a single chapter in the four Gospels where Jesus is not reported as doing something miraculous — walking on the water, feeding thousands of people on next-to-no food, healing the sick and even raising them from the dead. What is more, similar things are reported in the Acts of the Apostles as being done by the early disciples. We all know that a belief in miracles has always been a central item in Christian tradition. And yet — if we are really honest — most of us would have to admit that we are rather bothered about it; we can't altogether make sense of it, and we're not very happy about it.

Just the same applies to visions. St. Paul sees a vision on the road to Damascus, and it changes his whole life. Stephen sees a vision as he is about to be stoned to death because of his belief in Christ, and his face seems to shine like an angel's. What on earth are these visions?

What is true of the New Testament in these things applies also to the Old Testament; but the problem is worse. Did the walls of Jericho really fall down after the Children of Israel had solemnly marched round them and blown a trumpet? Did Elijah disappear into the clouds in some sort of heavenly chariot? Did the widow's cruse of oil really never run dry? What does it mean that the boy Samuel had visions when he was one of the servants of Eli the High Priest in the Temple? We are very unhappy about many of these things. Must we believe them?

There are several reasons for this uncertainty. And let me say straight off, that it's far better to be honest about our misgivings, and not try to force ourselves into some sort of irrational and uncritical belief. One of the major problems with us is that these things don't seem to happen in the twentieth century. Once, when Jesus had just finished healing someone, the crowd all round him cried out: 'We never saw it in this fashion'. We can say just the same thing. We don't see miracles every day of our lives. In addition to this some of the miracles frankly don't seem to fit.

There was once a barren fig tree which had leaves, but no fruit. We are told that Jesus cursed it. He said 'No man shall eat fruit of thee hereafter' — and it promptly withered away. Now I must say that this seems all wrong to me; it just doesn't square with the deep love of nature which Jesus shows in other places. If it is true, it seems very unlike him.

But perhaps most of all, miracles appear to contradict scientific laws. With the possible exception of the miracles of healing (about which we understand a lot more now than we used to) they run counter to our knowledge of the world, which science has gained for us. People *don't* walk on the water as Jesus is reported to have done on the lake near Capernaum: people don't change water into wine as he did at the marriage feast at Cana in Galilee, and we are not accustomed to look for the resurrection of the dead. These things don't happen, and we are inclined to believe that they can't happen, because, if they did, it would make nonsense of all scientific laws and we should not know what to believe about anything.

So also with visions. If someone claims to be having visions today he might be put into a mental home, and doctors might say he suffers from delusions. Moreover, such religious delusions seem more common than any other sort.

All these are real difficulties, which have made us far less sure about miracles than our fathers and grandfathers used to be. In those days the truth of the miracles was accepted without much criticism. In fact they were used as the starting point in lots of Christian argument. 'If the Bible is true, miracles and visions did occur, so Jesus Christ was divine . . . ' But now things have changed completely; we no longer argue from miracles, but to them. Many people, including sincere Christians, regard them as a liability, almost an encumbrance that distracts us from the real central message of the New Testament. And when people claim their existence today we get embarrassed.

I remember, in 1940, during World War II, how the retreating British army gathered on the beaches of Dunkirk. There was a tremendous sea operation, in which hundreds of little boats came over from Folkestone and Dover and all along that part of the South Coast, and brought them back to the safety of English soil. The whole operation was feasible because there was sufficient fog so that the German Air Force could not see what was happening; and moreover the sea remained quite calm so that even little motor boats could make the Channel crossing in safety. This whole incident was often referred to as a miracle, implying that

God had ordered the fog and the calm weather in order that British soldiers could be brought back out of danger. But I never heard this sort of description without being very worried. Why should God treat the British army better than the French or the Belgian? Very few people today would want to claim that all the responsibility for causing the Second World War was German, or that all British soldiers were angels! To claim this as a miracle seems awfully like claiming God as a British ally — almost a return to the tribal God of the early part of the Old Testament. Did not Christ come to show that God was father of all people everywhere? It doesn't make sense to put this in national uniform. We had better be careful before we claim the existence of miracles today. And anyhow, we are almost on the point of being able to forecast the weather for a week or so ahead. Is it seriously suggested that this fog and calm sea could not have been predicted in advance, before the retreat began? If it could have been predicted, how is it a miracle? If it could not have been predicted, and the North Sea gales ought to have been raging instead, wouldn't that make nonsense of all serious study of the weather? Would not science itself be a rather futile waste of time? We might as well go back to the tribal witch-doctors and medicine men; or to the old Greek oracle at Delphi where — for a consideration — your future would be 'revealed' to you.

If we want to deal sensibly with this question of miracles and visions we shall have to distinguish between the Old and the New Testament. The real difficulties lie in the New Testament and not in the Old. To begin with, parts of the Old Testament were written a very long time ago: they describe man's growing knowledge of God: contemporary literature shows that figurative language was as much the rule as the exception. (When the courtier said: 'O King, live for ever', he didn't mean it, for he was speaking in the manner of the time and place concerned.) Truth was wrapped up in story form — sometimes for safety. If Joseph had told his family the plain truth of his 'dreams', they would not merely have sold him into slavery in Egypt, they would have made sure that there was no·Joseph left alive to be their ruler! Ideas of scientific truth had not developed at that time; and no one worried about it. As a result it is extraordinarily difficult to sort out literal fact from the clothing in which it is wrapped up. Even the experts — the Old Testament scholars who spend their lives studying and comparing one writing with another — are uncertain. We really must not let the curious miraculous events of the Old Testament worry us. One day perhaps we shall have a greater ability than now to sift what is historically true from what is not. In the meanwhile it should be sufficient to recognize this difficulty, to treat the Old Testament as a record of God's progressive revelation of himself, and of man's slow acceptance of what God is really like. Many of the details do not matter, though it is reassuring that there are several cross-references that agree with other accounts of some of the main events. If you want to invent an explanation of some of these Old Testament miracles there is nothing wrong in doing so, provided that you don't insist that you're absolutely right about it! For example, if you want to believe that the walls of Jericho fell down because of an earthquake, I don't see why you shouldn't do so: but you must not say that your friend is a liar if he tells you that he thinks they fell down because as the Children of Israel marched round the city, all the inhabitants crowded on to the walls to see what was happening, with the result that too great a weight was put on them, and they gave way. The truth is that we don't know exactly why it happened — nor even whether the whole or a part of the walls collapsed. The sensible policy is to reserve our judgement — in the true sense of the word, to be agnostic. For 'agnostic' means saying 'I do not know': it is a very different attitude of mind from that when we say: 'it was just like this', or 'it did not occur at all'. There is nothing un-Christian about this sort of conclusion, and for many of us it is the only honest way. It still leaves us completely free to recognize those things which really are important in the Old Testament — man's developing knowledge of God; his failings and God's re-acceptance of him; the sense of God as creator and sustainer of the physical world, and the tremendous importance of bringing together the spiritual and the material. None of these is dependent upon a literal acceptance of the Old Testament miracles and visions.

But it is different with the New Testament. For this was written more recently: we have better manuscripts of the original text: a great deal more is known about contemporary historical events: much more clear-cut issues arise, and they are in thought-forms that come much closer to our own. In this respect we have got to look much more seriously and carefully into the New Testament than into the Old Testament.

I can only see three alternatives open to us. If we face up to the situation described in the New Testament we have got either (1) to disbelieve them as being false accounts of what actually happened, or (2) to explain them away by showing, if we can, that despite appearances, they don't really contradict scientific laws, or else (3) we must accept them. Let me say something about each of these in turn, realizing that we are not forced to accept the same alternative for all the New Testament visions and miracles. We may even conclude that we need all three options, as well as the agnostic one mentioned earlier, if we are to play fair both with ourselves and with the Bible. Only when we have sorted this out can we really deal with the twentieth-century situation.

First we may disbelieve them. People have tried to wipe out all miracles from the gospel stories. They have imagined that you could go through the New Testament with a pair of scissors, cutting out what you didn't like, and then trying to believe what you had got left. In a limited sense this can be done; but only in a limited sense. The plain fact is that things don't work so easily as that — the baby goes out with the bath water — and what is left is not Christianity. It is a collection of bits of good advice associated with a God who is not unlike Father Christmas. Such a faith has no real drive in it, and, as recent study of the original documents has shown pretty definitely, it isn't playing fair with what the writers of these original documents honestly believed. But — what is worse still — if you snip out certain parts of the New Testament, what is to stop you going further? You might just as well choose precisely those parts you do like, and put the rest in the wastepaper-basket. The result will be a nice, pleasant, easy, comfortable sort of religion, which won't worry anyone, or cause offence to anybody. The trouble is: it won't do much good either: and it just will not be Christianity.

However, such wholesale disbelief is not necessary. We are always at liberty to use our intelligence. We can ask about a particular miracle or vision: 'Is it in keeping with what we learn of Christ or his disciples in the rest of the New Testament?' If it is in keeping — in character, as we might say — then we ought to consider it seriously, whether or not we happen to like it. If it is not in character, we can be agnostic and reserve our judgment. In my own case this would apply to the fig tree alleged to have been cursed by our Lord. I remain agnostic because it just doesn't fit with other more important things that I know about him. I am much more inclined to suspect that the incident never really occurred at all; it was part of one of the wonderful stories that he was always telling; and years later, when the gospel came to be written and the details of events were getting a bit hazy in people's minds, only part of the story was remembered, and even that part was set down as an event and not a story. There was

probably a gap of several decades after our Lord's death before
even the earliest records were actually written. It would not be
surprising if in the mouth-to-mouth repeating of those early days
some confusion of the sort occurred. If I take this view — as, in
this case, I do — there is one very important point to remember.
It is my view, and not necessarily other people's, nor even
necessarily correct. I must not insist that other folk accept it also.

This leads to the second possibility — of explaining miracles
away and showing that they don't really contradict scientific law.
Some people have tried to do this with all the miraculous element
of the New Testament. I can show you what I mean if I give you
a so-called 'explanation' of the resurrection of our Lord, which I
have both heard, and read in a reputable book. According to this
idea, the physical body did in fact disintegrate, bit by bit, and the
individual atoms, like the separate atoms of a gas, moved to and
fro all round that cave in the rock of Joseph of Arimathea's
garden, until they found the tiny space between the opening of
the cave and the edge of the stone that had been rolled in front.
There would, quite certainly, be sufficient room between the two
for the atoms to diffuse to the outside. Once they were there,
they could reassemble and form the risen body. I will not now go
into the details of the extent to which all this is strictly possible
on a scientific basis. For I am bound to say that the whole thing
would then be so improbable and so theatrical that I should find
it very hard to accept.

You can do the same sort of thing with most of the other
miracles. But what you end up with is not the God and Father of
Jesus Christ, but a first-rate conjuror, or a kind of super-juggler,
who has got sufficient sleight-of-hand to do things we cannot do,
and who cheats us into believing that he can break all the laws of
science when all the time he isn't really breaking them. I said
earlier that some of the recorded miracles did not seem to fit the
life and character of Jesus. This sort of thing would fit much
worse: and it is rather horrid.

But it may be a way out for some of the healing miracles, and
for some of the visions. We know a lot more now than we used to
know about the relationship between mind and body. We know a
little about the strange powers that some people seem to possess
over the minds and bodies of some others. Faith healing is not
possible for everyone, but it certainly is possible for some. And it
need not deny medical science (even though some of those who
practise it seem anxious to claim that it does!). I do not find it
surprising that when a young man was brought to our Lord, and

that penetrating gaze of his rested on him, and that extraordinary insight into the deep parts of the young chap's whole being was put into operation, our Lord could say: 'Son, thy sins are forgiven; arise and walk.' I will go so far as to say that if I had that same power of penetrating human disguise, and that same insight into human character, I believe that I could say: 'arise and walk'. The point here is that since I do not have such insight, and my own grasp of spiritual things does not approach his, I cannot do what he did. The miracle — if indeed the word miracle is to be used — is that Jesus Christ was the sort of person that he most evidently was. When someone like that comes into our experience all that we can say is that, without all the business of scientific evidence and scientific proof, we are aware of a higher science, which does not contradict our very human science, but which goes beyond it. Perhaps, in the course of time, we may even learn enough about psycho-somatic relations as to be able ourselves to reproduce some of these 'miracles'. Visions also may come into this category, for the psychologists have told us of the extreme clarity with which some people can think and see ahead, especially in moments of great spiritual significance.

It would follow from this discussion that there may well be some miracles that we can accept fairly easily: and on semi-scientific evidence. But there remain others for which this explanation does not help. If we accept then it will have to be on the basis of non-scientific evidence. However, I don't think that this matters. Let me give an example.

If you ask me why I, as a professional scientist and a practising Christian, believe in the Resurrection, I shall reply that I believe in it on psychological and historical grounds — psychological because of the astounding effect that this event had on the disciples, and which could not conceivably have been 'put on', and is so evidently genuine: historical because it is a simple historical fact that the Christian Church has survived these 1900 years, far longer than any non-religious association of people, and this has been one of the central beliefs that has held it together. It is not a 'proof' of the Resurrection; but it is plain dishonesty to disregard evidence of this kind.

Another way of putting this argument is to say that there are other ways of describing our universe than scientific ones. Some people find this difficult to accept: but when you really think about it, it's clear that science is not — and never can be — a complete description of our experience as human beings. I am not trying to belittle science (this would hardly do for a science professor!), but I am trying to say that the scientific description of an event does not say everything that can be said about it. If I explain that an octave in music sounds pleasant because the frequencies of the two notes are exactly in the ratio of two to one, I may be giving a scientific description of what is meant by harmony: but I am certainly not saying all that a musician can say about it. If I claim that when people lose their tempers with each other there is an accelerated release of adrenalin into the blood, I am making a perfectly correct scientific observation: but it is hopelessly inadequate as a way of dealing with personal relationships, as we all know. If I watch the loving care with which a mother looks after her baby, I may describe it scientifically as one of the biological devices by which the race is preserved. I shall be quite right, but it would be preposterous to say that that was all there was to it. So, just because the scientific view of the world is not a complete one, we are at liberty to form our judgments on the basis of other types of evidence. The artist, the poet, the mystic, the historian, the theologian: all have their part to play in describing our world. None of them is complete: we need them all: we have no right to reject the evidence of any of them in an arbitrary way. What might seem to be a miracle to the scientist is everyday experience to the artist; and the poet knows a lot about visions.

If we can go this far, we come to the third of our earlier alternatives; which is to accept a fair proportion of the recorded miracles on the basis of largely non-scientific evidence. This does not by any means get rid of our difficulties. In some respects it makes matters worse, because we have agreed to accept events, at least some of which appear to be in flat contradiction with current scientific laws. This is a real dilemma. I cannot point to any way out of this dilemma which would be acceptable to every thoughtful Christian. But I can mention one of two things which help.

In the first place we must remember that science is always growing — that is half the fun in it. What is a scientific law today will possibly not be in twenty years' time. The old alchemists, for example, tried hard to change base metals into gold. They failed, and the effort to understand why they failed led to the atomic theory of the structure of matter. Atoms of different kinds exist: and as Clerk Maxwell, the Cavendish Professor of Physics at Cambridge, once said: systems may come and go, 'catastrophes may occur in the heavens', but the atoms and molecules 'out of which these systems are built — the foundation stones of the material universe – remain unbroken and unworn'. Anyone who claimed to have changed mercury into gold was indubitably a liar, for it was scientifically impossible. So much for 1873. In less than 100 years we have learnt how to smash these 'unbreakable' atoms into bits in a nuclear explosion, and to build them up again. There is hardly an atom of any kind which we cannot eventually change into any other kind, if we have enough money to buy the right apparatus. This does not mean that we have abandoned the atomic theory. It simply means that we have learnt when it is applicable, and when a 'miracle' shows that it is not. We could say that the old law of unchangeable atoms is now seen to be one part of a wider scientific law.

It may be like this with miracles. What appears now to conflict with scientific law may be seen quite differently as science develops. We may come to recognize times and situations when our present laws do not hold as rigorously as we sometimes think they do now. Such times would not be entirely unexpected if we associated them with a person possessing the same sort of spiritual power that Jesus obviously possessed. If our scientific knowledge did broaden out in this way, what is a miracle now to us would no longer be a miracle to our descendants. We should not speak of God 'interfering with the laws of science'. In fact some of our Lord's miracles might be reproducible by us and his words become true: 'the things that I do, ye shall do also: and greater things shall you do.'

But there is another way out of our difficulty. If it is true, as I said earlier, that the scientific way of looking at things is not the only valid one, and that there are other views, such as the poetic, the artistic and the religious, then there may be certain things that lie quite outside the scope of scientific enquiry. If there are such things, you cannot use science either to prove or disprove them. Now any event that cannot be reproduced cannot be discussed scientifically. For science is a means of correlating our observations; a scientific law only exists because, at some stage, we can more or less repeat our experiment and reproduce more or less the same result. If at no stage is there any chance of repeating the experiment, there will be no scientific law. As an example of this consider the original creation of the universe. Modern scientific research suggests that there was a critical moment, some ten to twenty thousand million years ago, beyond which scientific enquiry cannot penetrate. The scientific question: where did the atoms of matter come from? has no scientific meaning. We cannot reproduce this situation now, even in the

slightest significant degree. Science may be able to tell us when
the Creation took place. But there is not — and probably never
can be — a scientific theory, or law, of Creation.

What we call a miracle or a vision may be an event of this kind.
If so it does not discredit science, and we must not speak of God
interfering with the laws of science. Moreover our scientific study
of the world is unaffected by it. We could say that there is a
world of Nature (which is the scientific world), and also a world
of super-Nature. This latter world — as we often call it, the
supernatural world — cannot be experienced in scientific ways,
even though it impinges on the natural world. Christianity is not
the only religion to assert that such a world of super-Nature does
exist. All the great religions of the world believe it, and in
different ways they try to explain it. The words that they use are
words like revelation, the revealing of one world to another: and
inspiration; and forgiveness — many of which are exemplified for
us in the revelation of Jesus Christ. It is not therefore a question
of God interfering with the laws of science in the twentieth, or
any other, century. It is a question of recognizing the spiritual
world, and of responding to it.

I have just been outlining two ways of approaching miracles. If
you think carefully about them you will see that there is a good
deal which is common to them — the wider science within which
our present developing science is embedded: and the world of
super-Nature with which the world of Nature is encompassed. I
would not like to say that in these ways my difficulties in
understanding miracles are all resolved. But at least I can see that
the question with which this chapter is concerned, and which was
put at the beginning, is really a bogus question. In the first place
we are not compelled to believe in all the miracles and visions of
the Bible, and not even in all those reported in the New
Testament. And in the second place, the laws of nature are ways
of talking about certain aspects of the world, particularly the
reproducible ones, and there may well be other aspects not
covered in any sense by scientific laws. We come to scientific laws
by scientific enquiry and experiment. We may therefore expect to
come to understand these other situations quite differently, by
learning more about the spiritual world that interpenetrates the
world of Nature. For many of us the understanding of miracles
will come after, and not before, our growing into the Christian
faith, and then, oddly enough, we shall be far less worried about
this or that particular item than we now are. The early Christian
Justin Martyr put it all very simply, as long ago as the second

century A.D., 'there are some things which it is necessary to understand in order to believe' (that is science), 'and there are other things which it is necessary to believe in order to understand' (that is faith). Both attitudes are essential for the full development of a human being.

C. A. COULSON

What is God's attitude to atheists? If they lead good lives, do they go to heaven?

I am always chary of questions about the attitude of the Almighty to this or that. I have no individual 'hot line' to Heaven, and I am not fond of slick replies. Yet, people have the right to a straightforward and honest answer to a serious difficulty, and the difficulty framed above is certainly a serious one, and very relevant in our present society. Where there is question of a definitely revealed Christian truth, the matter is fairly simple. God has already spoken, and we have both the right and indeed the obligation to proclaim a firm answer. But when we start discussing the possible attitude of God to individual persons and groups of persons, we are well advised to proceed cannily. So many factors enter in, which we are scarcely in a position to assess and appreciate. And, after all, who are we to sit in judgment! In any case, better be canny — and slow! Such questions have to be examined against the whole background of Christian beliefs and principles, and the solution must emerge from the total pattern of Christian thought and experience. If and when we can manage to formulate it, it must be at once reasonable and in the fullest possible accord with what we know of the designs and purposes of God.

First, let us clarify this problem. Who are these atheists we are considering? *Atheists* are people who reject or will not accept *theism*. Now, *theism* is a rather exact concept. It does not include any kind of idea of any kind of god in any kind of vague and general way. You cannot stick the prefix 'pan' or 'poly' on to it, and keep what is meant by *theism*. The polytheism with which we are familiar in Greek mythology is not theism, unless the various gods and godesses are interpreted as manifestations or expressions of a single, higher Power or Person behind them all. The polytheist is, strictly, an *atheist*, not a *theist;* he may believe in half a hundred or half a thousand deities, he does not believe in the One God. In a similar way, a *pantheist*, for example in the Indian tradition, is no theist, although he has a real sense of spirit and spiritual values. Yet, in his eyes, Nature and God become fused and confused. Once everything is thought of as God, then nothing is any longer God. God is no longer envisaged as separate from this created world. Once again, the pantheist is, strictly, an *atheist*, and no *theist*.

Theism, more precisely, is the belief that there is a Supreme Power or Being, separate from and superior to, and completely transcending the world and universe of our experience. This Supreme Being is acknowledged as Creator, as having brought the universe into existence; it is because of his power, presence and providence that the universe continues to exist. In his relations with human beings, whom he has endowed with the qualities of reason and responsibility, he is sanction and Judge in the moral order. In the final resort, human beings are responsible before and to him. The ultimate standards of truth and morality are to be found in God.

This is the ordinary concept of religion, of man's recognition of and approach to God, as it is discovered in the varied and even primitive forms of man's expression. God is the Supreme Being, the Great Power, from whom man proceeds by some manner of creation, upon whom man is essentially dependent for existence, for good fortune and prosperity, and therefore towards whom he has certain obligations of acknowledgement, worship and service. This Supreme Being is the Highest Judge of human behaviour, a guardian of justice and morality, a Lord of pains, penalties and rewards. However crude and even distorted may be the setting, in some varieties of natural religion, these two basic notes are everywhere present. They are man's natural ascent and striving towards the Some-thing, the Some-one, above — beyond — transcending the limited sphere of his experience, and giving a more permanent sense and significance to that experience and to his life.

These two notions emerge so much more strongly and compellingly in the religion of the Jews, as we discover it in the Old Testament, with its intimate and continuing links between the One, True God, sharply and even fiercely distinguished from the false deities of surrounding nations, and both individual Jews and the entire Jewish people as a religious élite, consecrated to the worship and service of Jahweh. A similar concept runs through the Muslim tradition, while in Christian revelation it appears in greater depth and clearer detail, and the Supreme Being is conceived not only as divinely personal but as embracing the mystery of the Trinity, opening to man some insight into the life of God himself and enabling him to enter into a more intimate association with God.

Yet, to avoid ambiguity, this notion of *theism* has to be presented in a more comprehensive manner. In insisting upon the transcendence of God, the theist — and still less the Christian, is not suggesting that God has no connection or concern with the world. Far from it! That is how *deists* talked in the eighteenth century, for all they wanted from a Higher Principle was that someone must have started the world process going; once started, it could get along with its natural forces; there was no further need for Divine providence and God. But these deists were precisely not *theist;* they were in fact *atheists,* in the proper sense in which we are employing the term. With due respect to Dr. J. A. T. Robinson, the Christian does not picture a God *up there* or a God *out there,* remote from sublunary affairs. To use similar expressions, as he seems to do, about a God *down here* or a God *in* or *within us* would be just as absurd. If we apply spatial attributes to God, we do so because our language, like our experience which it expresses, is space- and time- conditioned, and we have to use it as best we can. When we declare that God is essentially transcendent, we mean that he is not involved substantially in the world process, which however depends at every moment upon his sustaining and upholding power. To be exact, God is *nowhere,* that is, he remains unaffected by spatial conditions. It would be equally correct to say that he is *everywhere,* for nowhere is his power and providence without effect. If God, in the theist and Christian view, transcends our world of Nature and experience, he is present to it, immanent within it, though always in substance distinct from it; it is not and never of the substance of God himself. But theism does not shoot the Supreme Being like a modern space-ship into the heavens, to remain there in detached and glorious isolation. It brings God down to earth, as manifesting himself in the qualities and details of his created world — in the shadows and images of Truth, Beauty and Goodness till the visible world itself can make us aware of God and teach us something of what he must be and indeed is; and as supporting, directing and renewing the world. To all created reality God is present, as the Lord of full reality, supporting and sustaining. God transcends but at the same time he is intimately present. Christian theism expresses itself equally well in the verse of the psalmist: 'Know ye that the Lord is God: it is he that made us, and we are his', and in the argument of St. Paul that it is in God that 'we live and move and have our being'.

In the second place, our approach to God is always wider than a logical conclusion. A man can indeed think the thing out, examine all the evidence, and conclude that there must be — and is — a Supreme Being. This is the reasoning that has run, almost uninteruptedly, through Western Philosophy until the nineteenth century. It would indeed be strange, the Christian would consider, that the Almighty had endowed mankind with the capacity for thought that was yet unable to recognize the existence and significance of God himself who had made the endowment. In fact, the special prerogative of man's mind is that it too has its own transcendence and can transcend the particular experiences of life in terms of general ideas and a larger pattern. The human mind seeks the universal through and in particulars, and thus transcends or rises above them. Only so, is man able to understand the design and relations of things; only so can he understand at all. In the final resort, all thought must end with what is *meta-physical*, with what lies behind the sphere of our day-to-day and here-and-now experience in this *physical* and *natural* world and which provides both the ground of its existence and its significance.

Even this does not take us the whole way. Man's approach to God is larger than logic. It is fundamentally an approach not only of the mind but of the man entire. The small measure of reality in man reaches out by an ontological instinct towards the Great Reality from which it derives. Man's heart, conscious that man's significance and destiny are not cribbed and cabined completely within the limits of this world, searches for that fuller satisfaction of mind and heart which the world from its own resources cannot supply. *Fecisti nos ad te, Domine* — that was the *cri du coeur* of St. Augustine. 'Lord, thou hast made us for thyself, and our hearts can find no rest until they rest in thee'. The acceptance of God — to prescind here from the further implications of Christian faith — is fuller and richer than intellectual assent. Formation, environment, cultural and national heritage, attachment and loyalties, personal experiences, gratitude, generosity and love — all have their part to play, so that the whole personality of man is involved. In the language of Pascal, it may well be that the *raisons du coeur*, which *raison*, in the narrower sense, cannot understand, speak here with grander eloquence and conviction.

The best or least inadequate parallel with genuine religion is human love. There is the same outgoing movement, away from the self, centred upon and in the object beloved. It is no chance that the first Christian commandment is that of love of God: not, mind you, adoration or worship or praise, though these are included and implied, but simply love, and a love that outsoars the notions of Almighty Power, All-knowing Mind, Loftiest Beauty and Supreme Being to rest on that of the Divine Goodness, for it is only goodness that is the final goal of love. And the goodness in question is that of a Heavenly Father, personally interested in and concerned about his children, with their truest welfare ever in mind, a Father providing generously despite their repeated ignorance, stupidity, ingratitude and failures. It is in the Christian revelation that we discover this goodness in its fullest and overwhelming expression: God's communication of his truth and life, in the person of Jesus Christ, the Son of God himself. Centuries of reflection on this revelation have taken us little, if at all, further than Christ's simple sentence, recorded by St. John: 'God so loved the world that he sent his only-begotten Son', and we might add from another scriptural context: 'Greater love than this' . . . not even God could have.

And now to return to the problem raised by the question at the head of this essay. What about the atheist? And what are we to think of his possibility or likelihood of salvation, for this is what the Christian means when he speaks of Heaven? For the Christian, the question is only one instance, albeit an extreme one, of the wider problem of salvation outside the Church of Christ. It is a problem that naturally has been discussed and debated through the centuries and to which, particularly in recent decades, a more flexible answer has been given. But are there still limits? Can the atheist — assuming a sincere conscience and good life on his part — be considered as within them?

If, as Christians, we attempt to work out an answer, it must be a theological one, not dictated by sentiment or some woolly slap-happy tenderness for all and sundry: it has to be based on certain principles.

The first of these principles is that a Christian stands fast by what he knows as revelation: God's communication of himself, his truth and life, through Jesus Christ. At a definite moment, eternity has entered into our historic time sequence. God has manifested himself. We have been redeemed through Christ and reconciled and associated in a wonderfully new manner with God. This happened once, and it happened once for all. Christian history is the working out of this unique act on God's part. Historically, this revelation brought us by Christ is handed on within Christ's Church. The Incarnation, the coming of Christ, was God's special incursion into time: that incursion is still operative in time within the Church. The New Testament shows us how Christ established this Church, giving it a universal mission, endowing it with his authority and strengthening it with his guarantee. The mission was universal; the apostles were sent out to *teach all peoples, commanding* them to accept that revelation. Christ's claims were absolute, as are those of the Church. The man who believes, Christ assures us, shall be saved; the man who refuses belief, will be condemned. Further, Christ realizes that some will reject him. He is, in the words of St. John, the light that shines in the darkness, which will not receive (or 'understand') him. The light has come into the darkness, Christ stresses this elsewhere, and men have preferred darkness to the light: for their works were evil, and could not 'stand up to' the light. Christ proclaims himself to be the Truth, the Life — and the Way, the Way that leads men to God, and he identifies 'eternal life' with a knowledge of the one, true God, the Father, and him whom the Father has sent, Jesus Christ.

In Christian eyes, then, Christ is the one and only Redeemer, for all mankind. Outside and apart from Christ there is and can be no salvation. For salvation is not a mere natural development; it is not progress of a naturally good person through a naturally good life to its culmination in a heavenly crown. To begin with, these supposedly good persons do not *naturally* exist. We know only of fallen and regenerated mankind. Man is redeemed by the sacrifice and triumph of Christ over sin and evil, and attachment to Christ through faith and baptism has reconciled man to God, and enriched his nature with a higher and spiritual capacity, by which he now lives with and to God. A new element enters in, that transcends the purely natural level and is a gift from God. Salvation comes to all men through Christ, and only through Christ. There is no substitute, no other way. Similarly, salvation continues to be brought to men through the Church of Christ: again, there is no other ultimate medium, no other absolute way. This used to be formulated severely in the expression, *Extra Ecclesiam nulla salus* (no salvation outside the Church) — severe indeed but still fundamentally correct, albeit understood in a far wider way. We are not asserting here that only believing Christians actually achieve salvation, though they alone have the opportunity of appreciating adequately the meaning of salvation and of realizing what an immense boon it is and how eloquent a guarantee of God's love. What we are insisting is that all those who do achieve salvation do so because of, and only because of, Jesus Christ — and in a similar measure, of the Church of Christ. How this can be so — is the theme of this essay. Supposing for the

moment that Buddhists, Hindus and even atheists are saved, they
are not saved because they are Buddhists or Hindus, but on
account of Jesus Christ, that same Jesus Christ, of whom
presumably they had little or next to no knowledge and certainly
no effective realization: as for the atheist, the situation is even
more difficult. If he is to be saved, this is not because he is an
atheist but most definitely in spite of the fact that he is an
atheist. He will be saved, in fact, in his own despite. All who
arrive at salvation, do so on account of Christ and his Church,
because they have been brought into some relation or association
with Christ.

The second basic tenet we must bear in mind in this discussion
is that of the will of God, that God wants all men to be saved.
That was why he created them. 'Salvation', that is association in
union and happiness with God after this sublunary life, is man's
ultimate destiny. *Fecisti nos ad te, Domine* – again, St. Augustine
expresses this truth. God is Omega as well as Alpha, Final purpose
and fulfilment as also Initial Source. Yet we remain inevitably
within an historic, that means time and place, situation, with its
inexorable limits. Christ, assuming our human nature, submitted
himself to these limitations. He became a man of a certain time
and place: his personal preaching was confined to the Holy land.
His Church has taught and missioned throughout the centuries,
but again with the same limitations of geography and history, and
the even more subtle barriers of language, tradition, psychology
and alien culture. After nineteen centuries it has made scant
inroad into the teeming countries of the Far East. What is our
reaction to this? Are we to suggest that these peoples that have
had little or no contact with Christ and his Church are beyond
salvation? That surely would be to make a sheer mockery of
God's salvific design! Yet we cannot abandon our first principle,
which is the lynchpin of all Christian thinking: all salvation is
because of Jesus Christ. How is this to be harmonized with the
fact of these immense numbers that know nothing or next to
nothing about Christ as the one Saviour!

This theological problem is of course not new. We have come a
long way from the atmosphere of the early ballads, in which
chrétiens ont droit, païens ont tort, and even then the actual
relations between Christians and Saracens and Moors were a good
deal more flexible than their theological opinions. It was the
difficulty for Catholic theologians concerning their non Catholic
Christian brethren, if the Church of Christ was to be equated with
the historic Catholic Church; the answer was easier here because

of baptism, common to both, and an area of common faith in spite of disagreements.

But what of the non-Christian? Let us be clear. We are considering people who are in good faith and conscience: not such as, Christian or non-Christian, repudiate God either deliberately or because they have immersed themselves in a purely material existence. We are thinking of the people to whom the Christian gospel has never been effectively brought. How can they be saved — if our first principle has to be accepted, namely, that all salvation is through Christ. How can they be saved through a name and person they have not known! The reply has to be sought in the second principle, that of God's will, that he wants all men to be saved. If God wants all men to be saved, he must provide the opportunity and overcome the limitations of the historic situation. God — theologians hold — offers to every man his grace — he works upon his mind, directs and inspires him, and leaves him with the decision: is he to follow out what he understands to be right, to shoulder and fulfil his obligations, avoid sin and evil, and indeed carry out what, in however vague and as yet undeveloped a way, he acknowledges to be God's will? Theologians have long considered that man in this frame of mind, encouraged and assisted by Divine grace, wishes to fulfil the Divine Will, and therefore equivalently to receive the truth of Christ, had it but been made clear to him, and sacramental baptism. Theologians have spoken of this implicit readiness as a *baptism of desire* (the expression 'desire of baptism' might have been a happier one), and treat it as a substitute for, though not the full equivalent of, sacramental baptism.

More recent theology has extended this interpretation. With these men of good faith (we are dealing with these) they discover in their response to God's grace a *votum ecclesiae*, that is a wish or willingness to enter the Church of Christ. They know for the most part nothing about this Church; if they are Asians, it may in their eyes be associated with the hegemony of the white man, with exploitation and colonialism. None the less, they are reacting properly to and corresponding with God's grace and invitation. Limited and in part distorted though their view of God may be, they desire to fulfil his will and live moral and fully human lives. They want — implicitly and seriously — to do whatever God is asking of them: and this, ideally or even factually, if it has been brought home to them, includes membership of the historic Church of Christ. They are thus related to this Church, *by desire,* though not of course actually.

Some theologians refer to them as *anonymous* Christians, members of the Church because of their response to grace (which after all, is always the *gratia Christi*, the grace of redemption won by Christ), if not by explicit acceptance. Other theologians go further and speak of this *anonymous* path of salvation as in fact the ordinary way. Explicit faith and professing membership of the Church is the privilege of only a minority of mankind, that has obligations corresponding with its privileges.

This attitude is encouraged to-day by the change of Christian approach to non-Christian faiths. The earlier tendency was to regard them as false. Missionaries aimed at converting the 'benighted heathen' from darkness to light. Christian opinion now, witness the relative decrees of the Vatican Council, finds in these religions much that is crude, false, distorted and incomplete but recognizes at the same time valuable elements, revealing the true God, and signifying the action of God on the peoples concerned through these various faiths: they are seen as opening men's minds to God and the Divine will and purpose and thus preparing them for a fuller acceptance of Divine revelation. This approach looks upon them much as the Church of the fourth and fifth centuries envisaged the moral, religious and cultural heritage of ancient Greece and Rome, as a *praeparatio evangelica*, a preparation for the Christian gospel. Plato could be honoured as a 'Moses speaking Greek', and Virgil and the Sibyls reverenced as pagan equivalents of the prophets of Israel.

But — you may ask — does this net, as finely-meshed and far-flung as you have made it, really gather in the atheist? If the salvation of non-Christians is made to depend upon some response to the grace of God, and therefore some recognition of God himself, how can it apply to the atheist, who presumably is rejecting God altogether? It is by no means easy to answer this objection, especially as we maintain that the human mind, by natural reason alone, can, and therefore should, recognize God's existence. But remember, we are not here dealing with rebels against God's authority or with men so occupied with worldly affairs that they can find neither inclination nor time to consider spiritual questions, nor indeed with apostles and propagandists for a godless atheism. The key phrase in the introductory question is 'who lead good lives', and this supposes a genuine sincerity. The 'good lives' in question clearly imply a clear recognition of right and wrong, a steady determination to carry out the former and avoid the latter, with a serious sense of self-respect and duty, and a careful feeling of responsibility, justice and goodness towards others. Anything short of this can scarcely be deemed a 'good life'.

There are two factors in the modern outlook and situation that have greatly affected the problem of the 'atheist' (incidentally, 'agnostic' would often be a better term). The first is the development in modern philosophy since Kant, which supposes that the human mind is limited to the knowledge of *phenomena*, to what is presented through sense experience. Kant's acceptance of God is through faith, not reason. The tendency is even more strongly evident in Positivism – a useful scientific approach, no doubt, but a restrictive and miserable philosophy – which limits our knowledge to the data of this-world experience and denies to us the possibility of transcending it. This removes the 'meta' from 'physics'. All that we can know is the physical universe: this can be weighed and measured, ticketed and registered, but we cannot go beyond. . . . ! But God is essentially beyond: he is therefore outside our realm of knowledge.

This concentration on the world, the 'here and now' has been forcibly accentuated by the rapid and amazing development of modern technology, by man's growing control and mastery of Nature. In earlier ages, it is argued, men may have needed the providence of God, at least as a supporting idea and ideal. Advances have been so great that man is now his own providence. He can now assume the mantle which he formerly attributed to God. In other words, man has grown to adulthood, he has come into his own. Finally, it is encouraged by certain groups of Christian writers who seem anxious to reduce all religion to sheer ethics, to replace the first commandment of Christ, that of the love and service of God, almost exclusively by the second, that of love and service of the neighbour, and by the handful of fringe Christian advocates of the 'Death of God' theology, for whom in view of modern man's maturity, God has either abdicated or become irrelevant.

It is in this new atmosphere that Western society is living to-day, and in particular the scientist and specialist. It provides his methods of approach to his work, it bounds his horizon. God is outside it, as he envisages it; God is accordingly unreal or irrelevant. Making allowance for this, can we still argue that such a man, leading the 'good life' that is postulated, has, in spite of his explicit or implicit rejection of God, still some basic awareness, of which he is not – at least not fully – conscious? Does the recognition of right and wrong, the practical implementation of this recognition throughout his life, not point to some basic, though concealed, awareness of the God who is the sanction of the moral order and its Final Judge? Does not the sustained effort to live in conformity with human nature, understood as reasonable and responsible, not suppose again the recognition of the Supreme Creator? If so, may we not speak of a relation (contradictory enough, it would naturally appear) between the man whose attitude is denial of God, and the very God whom that attitude expressly repudiates?

I am not proposing this as a complete and certain answer but indicating lines along which Christian theologians are thinking. In any solution, the two polarities have to be brought together: the fact that salvation is through and only through Christ, and the salvific will of God. What response, under these or the other circumstances, on the part of man may be deemed adequate, is a further matter which, in the final resort, belongs to the mysterious assessments of God himself.

JOHN MURRAY, S.J.

What sort of a person was Jesus?

The birth of Jesus meant that to help and redeem the human race, which had disappointed all his hopes and had played havoc with his world, God deliberately involved himself in the human situation. This involvement meant that, taking the form of man, he had himself to experience not the best that life can give us, but the very worst that it can do to us. Thus he was born in the squalor of a country tavern's stable, mid-way between the Eastern and the Western worlds, lived with superb gallantry, and a supporting sense of humour with which he is not always credited, a life in which every conceivable social circumstance was against him, experienced the grim frustration of poverty, endured the viciousness of human spite and hatred, and knew also the bitterness of the disloyalty of friends.

He gathered about him a small and strangely assorted handful of people — among them were some tough Galilean fishermen, a revenue official in the employment of the detested Roman Government, and a cultivated young man of the Jerusalem upper classes. Mesmerized by his moral and spiritual grandeur and his radiant personality, these men were prepared to accept the difficulties attendant upon close personal association with him. After their own fashion they loved him; but at the supreme crisis of his life they deserted him to a man. He was submitted on all sides to intolerable humiliations. He was thwarted by the Church and intrigued against by the leaders of the State. For a time he was popular with some sections of society which, as always, were eager to sponsor an unusual personality, but who soon dropped him when his spiritual power and moral incorruptibility became too inconvenient for their continued patronage. The message he preached of the universal Fatherhood of God and the brotherhood of men, irrespective of nation, colour, caste, or creed; his insistence that all mankind were equal in privilege and responsibility before their Maker; his extension of the divine grace and love to all the human race, and his proclamation of the Kingdom of God as demanding allegiance above and beyond all earthly dominion made him profoundly suspect with both the leaders of the Jewish Church and the Roman administration. Eventually they managed to get him arrested on trumped-up charges. He was tried and condemned to death with monstrous illegality, and then was executed, after the fashion of the time, by being nailed alive on two cross-beams of wood. His gallant young life went out in darkness and in apparent utter defeat. Just another obscure individual added to the thousands who had ended their lives on crosses on the hill called Golgotha, or the place of skulls.

And yet . . . and yet? It wasn't the end: something very strange happened. The little group who had deserted him at his death now came forward asserting that on the third day after his execution Jesus had appeared to them alive. They not only asserted this extraordinary happening, but they started out to devote their lives to declaring it. He was alive, and death had had no dominion over him. Now, we have to face up to this question — did these men now dedicate themselves to proclaiming as a fact something that was going to lead each one of them to martyrdom and a hideous death, but which in their hearts they knew was nothing but a lie?

At Christmastime, round the civilized earth, rises a mighty chorus of worship and adoration as Christian men go in their dreams to Bethlehem. What came to pass there, and what, some thirty-three years later, happened at and after Calvary that gave rise to this incredible conviction that, in Jesus, God himself came amongst us? There may be some reading this who may have drifted from any allegiance to the Christian Church, or who have grown perhaps a little cynical or superior in their attitude towards it, or to whom Christianity has become so conventional that they have really never thought about it at all. I would ask them if they would in honesty and reverence try to think out an answer to that question, for it is far too big and too commanding for any of us to push it aside.

> Who is He in yonder stall,
> At whose feet the shepherds fall?

Well, let us try to conjure up for ourselves a picture of the man this child was to grow to be. We are so accustomed in our thoughts to associate Jesus with a city like Jerusalem, or a town like Capernaum, that we tend to forget how much at heart he was a countryman. His love of the country glows through all his parables. He looks on field and tree and river and flower as only a country-lover could do.

To the eyes of the young, the wonders of the countryside and the beauties of nature, the very minutest details in field and river and hedgerow, have a clarity and significance which the passing of the years seems somehow to corrode and dim. Wordsworth, you remember, felt this very keenly. Recalling his childhood's attitude to the natural world he confessed that

> There was a time when meadow, grove, and stream,
> The earth, and every common sight,
>   To me did seem
>   Apparelled in celestial light,
> The glory and the freshness of a dream.

But now, he added, 'there hath passed away a glory from the earth.' And Charles Dickens once said that the magic of spring to the grown man who had early memories of the countryside was that it transported him back to the scenes of his childhood.

Have you ever noticed that our Lord was one to whom those scenes of childhood remained permanently fresh? He consistently preserved that childlike interest in the smallest things and happenings of common life, that sympathy with all sorts of people which made the whole world his home and all men his brethren, and all the birds and the beasts his friends. His greatest teachings are never expressed in theological or metaphysical phraseology. They are phrased in simple words and are based on the memories of the scenes of his childhood in the Galilean countryside.

'Consider the lilies how they grow'. Where first did he see lilies, but on the slopes of the hills round Nazareth? His most significant and telling illustrations are culled from humdrum daily life in that poor man's house where he spent his early years. The great truths of God and man, and life and death, are spoken in terms of candles and moths, and rust and bushels (that is, measures of grain or fruit) and bread-baking in the oven, and lost coins rolling under the kitchen dresser — a very serious matter for very poor people! — and sowing and reaping, and searching the hillside for sheep that had strayed. What exciting times he must have had as a boy, roaming the hillsides with those remarkable Eastern shepherds who knew every sheep by name, and who were always having to rid their flocks of the wild goats that were constantly invading them. And in later years he remembers — 'The good shepherd calleth his sheep by name.' . . . 'Separating the sheep from the goats.'

He preached as one who remembered what it was like to be young, who never lost his alert and vivid interest in everyday affairs, and to whom the world was permanently fresh. That was why the ordinary people heard him gladly. He didn't preach in the ponderous scholarly language of the great Rabbis in the Temple at Jerusalem, forever expounding the Law and the Prophets, or in the controversial manner of the Pharisees and the Sadducees, hating each other like poison because they disagreed on points of doctrine. He didn't use the sort of talk the people heard in their local synagogues. He talked in language that ordinary folk could understand.

Did he want to bring home to men the dark and tragic waywardness of the human will? He tells them of children playing in the market place, as he himself had so often done at Nazareth; and the game goes all to bits and everything is spoiled because some of them turned sulky and said they wouldn't play. What a parable is there! The bountiful goodness of God is illustrated not by the glories of Solomon, but by the lilies which as a boy he plucked in the fields of Galilee. The divine omnipotence of him who sits upon the throne of the universe is revealed not by reference to armaments and national wealth, and crusading despots, but to the birds of the air whose Heavenly Father feeds them. Would he illustrate the vastness of his conception of the Kingdom of God? He finds his metaphor in a grain of mustard seed, or in a fisherman's net. And for the fundamental truth of the unity of man with himself, and himself with God, he thinks of the vines which grew on the hillsides of Palestine — 'I am the true Vine, and you are the branches.' Would he try to get them to understand the rejection by the world of God's proffered love in himself? — He remembers the foxes which had their holes about Nazareth, and the birds whose nests he often looked for — but he has nowhere to lay his head. Or again, he would try to impress on his hearers the reality of the Holy Spirit — well, he thought of the evenings in the long-gone days, perhaps when the villagers gossiped about the village well and the twilight wind crept up the village street, now coming, now going, over the fields among the corn, no man knew how or whence. So also is the Spirit of God.

It is all so homely, so real. It is religion in common life, where men and women worked, got into difficulties, loved, sorrowed, sinned, repented. In all those immortal sermons in Capernaum and Jerusalem, the Man who spoke them went back on the wings of dreams to his childhood and the Galilean hamlet which he loved; to the world of nature and the open countryside, and the life of the birds and beasts of the field, and of simple men and women, where he had first learned the reality of God.

There is no interpreter of the countryside like Jesus. He looks into flower and tree and blossom with such penetrating insight. He sees the wayside violet, the snow-white lambs, the sparrow on the housetop, the cattle on a thousand hills, as protected and upheld in the security of the living God. He teaches us to associate the name of Infinite Love with everything in nature which delights our eyes and gladdens our hearts. His unfaltering trust in the goodness of God fills the valleys with music and the hills with song, and lights the sparkling waters. Christianity, never forget, is a contagious thing. You catch it from other people. No man was ever yet converted by a Gifford Lecture, as one of my old professors used to say!

How do you think that a movement started two thousand years ago by a little group of obscure people in Palestine, who went about saying that in a young Galilean peasant they had found God's perfect witness to himself — that this Jesus was alive and that through the power of his presence in their own lives they had literally become new creatures — how do you think that what these people said began a movement which, within a few centuries, was to supplant the Roman Empire? There were no telephones, no newspapers, no wireless, no television; no mass media or any means of rapid communication. The first of the Gospels was not written until some thirty years after the Crucifixion; the Epistles, or Letters, of St. Paul and other New Testament writers were sent to already established Christian communities in such widely scattered places as Rome, Corinth, Ephesus, Philippi, Galatia, Thessalonika. Christianity had already spread through personal contacts. People had become converted to it because of what they saw was happening to other people's lives and characters because of their faith in Jesus Christ.

So we shall find, if we seek, in its all too swiftly passing hours the secret of the indwelling peace, and thus we will go on with faith and hope and courage. The years are passing and each one is bringing us nearer to the great solution of all mysteries. Some day for each one of us the light will glow more clear.

It is he before whom men kneel in adoration here in time who is the revelation of that love of God which will surround and bless and lead us still hereafter in eternity, and whose dominion in this and in whatever world our souls may penetrate must for ever continue to endure.

CHARLES L. WARR

Does Jesus still exist?

My first comment is to suggest that it is by no means of the same order as the questions — 'Does Socrates still exist?' 'Does Shakespeare still exist?' Nor does it go into the same category as the question — 'Do our loved ones who have passed through death still exist?'

Quite clearly the question, as asked, is not just an inquiry about a hypothetical immortality of influence nor even about personal survival. Socrates undoubtedly still exists in the philosophical tradition which he inherited from his predecessors and proceeded to recreate, a tradition which is fruitful and alive to this very day. Shakespeare certainly still exists in the marvellous insight into life and character which has gone on working dynamically from the Elizabethan age until now. Nor is theirs merely this kind of immortality of influence, such as George Eliot aspired to:

> Oh may I join the choir invisible
> Of those immortal dead who live again
> In lives made better by their presence.

For Socrates and Shakespeare themselves, we may confidently believe, survive in that unseen realm in which those we call the departed are gathered, that dimension of eternity in which our own loved ones who have passed from mortal sight are living now.

But this question, 'Does Jesus still exist?' is different. What is involved here is not the producing of evidence that personality can survive death and continue to live on in a world unseen. For Jesus is not just another of the world's illustrious teachers, nor is he one more martyr gone heroically to his reward. There are some lines of John Drinkwater that express the difference:

> Shakespeare is dust, and will not come
> To question from his Avon tomb,
> And Socrates and Shelley keep
> An Attic and Italian sleep.

They see not. But, O Christians, who
Throng Holborn and Fifth Avenue,
May you not meet, in spite of death,
A traveller from Nazareth?[1]

Here we meet the real crux of the inquiry. Behind the
question, 'Does Jesus still exist?' lies the challenge demanding an
answer: 'Is Christ alive today? Is he in a unique way our
contemporary? Does he in some unparalleled manner reveal his
living presence in the Church and the world, in history and
individual experience? Can we still meet and encounter this
'Traveller from Nazareth'? Does God speak to us in Christ in the
here and now? May we be so united with the living Christ that his
Spirit permeates our own, and his risen life becomes ours?'

II

In seeking to answer these questions, our starting-point is
clear. It is the Resurrection. Christ, says Paul, was 'declared to be
the Son of God with power, according to the Spirit of holiness,
by the resurrection from the dead.'[2]

If it should be asked, But can you prove the resurrection? we
must begin by answering that it is not possible to effect a
scientifically compulsive demonstration, in the sense of coercing
the intellect of each and every man who considers the evidence.
You will never 'prove' Christianity like that. In this connection, is
it not significant that the Gospels never represent the risen Christ
as having appeared to any except to disciples and believers? This,
indeed, is a fact on which many critics have been quick to pounce
as justifying their scepticism. Why did he not appear to Caiaphas
or Herod? What a dramatic confrontation that would have been!
Why not to scribes and Pharisees, Romans and Greeks? Would not
such a return from the dead have confounded all opposition and
compelled belief? No, it would not. 'If they hear not Moses and
the prophets, neither will they be persuaded though one rose
from the dead.'[3] And today, if someone sets out with the dogma
that miracles do not happen and that therefore the resurrection is
impossible – the visionary hallucination of the disciples, or the
fantastic figment of early Christian imagination, the Church
inventing the faith by which it was to live – it is unlikely that any
amount of argument will move him. But what is happening in
such a case is that the man's philosophical presuppositions are
disqualifying him for the task of historian. The fact is that for
any unbiassed responsible investigator, seeking seriously to

cultivate objectivity, the evidence in its own right is immensely impressive.

Let us consider that evidence now. There are the appearances to the disciples, as cited by Paul in 1 Corinthians 15: 3–8, a passage derived by the apostle from a very primitive, pre-Pauline source. There are the narratives in the Gospels themselves. There, it is true, the appearances are described with certain discrepancies. But these, so far from diminishing the historical credibility of the narratives, lend them a verisimilitude which no amount of manipulated consistency could have given. There is, further, the fact of the empty tomb. Would the authorities have failed to produce the body of Jesus, and thus to refute the disciples' story and strangle the strange tale at its birth, had they been able to do it?

Further, and on a different level, there is the fact of the sudden miraculous transformation of the disciples from a group of cowed and disillusioned and despairing men into a fellowship aflame with joy and victory, their voices resonant, their words ringing like iron, their souls defying fear. They and their successors who lived and wrote in the generation after Jesus had passed from sight were sure he was alive and active still. When they broke bread in their Eucharists on the first day of the week, they were not harking back to a past now gone for ever; and when they prayed at the Eucharist, 'Come, Lord'[4] it meant not only a remote Second Advent, not only 'Come, Lord, at the consummation of the age', but 'Come, Lord, now, come to us gathered here in worship, come to this Eucharist in all thy risen power.'

Take the greatest of them all, St. Paul himself. I have heard his conversion described in terms of neurosis, epilepsy, brain-washing! I submit that such explanations are fantastically remote from beginning to account for the magnificently balanced, heroically courageous life of the apostle. The only possible explanation is the man's own: at Damascus he had been confronted by the risen living Christ, and that confrontation had led on to a daily renewed fellowship with his Lord of such intensity that he could say — 'I live, yet not I, but Christ liveth in me.'[5]

And so it has been right down the centuries. There is the fact of the continued life of the Church, and the evidence of the working of the living Lord through all subsequent generations and amongst people of all nations and tongues. Is it credible that all this stems from a concocted tale and is founded on a myth?

What I am seeking to emphasize is that even for the

professional historian, apart from faith altogether, such evidence has indubitable value and must be treated with respect. It is a mark of the scientific historian that he is always prepared to allow for new unprecedented factors emerging on to the scene. Must we not say that in the person of Jesus it was precisely this that had happened? An unprecedented factor was present. He was one of ourselves, as the Epistle to the Hebrews poignantly insists; yet his life was unlike any other that has ever appeared on earth. It was not simply that here was genius raised to the highest degree of explosive originality. Here was a life of a different order altogether.

It will help to clarify this if we consider the claims he made for himself. He does not say, like Socrates and other great world teachers, 'The truth is everything, I am nothing': he says, 'I am the truth.' Though the meekest of all the sons of men, he can tell his enemies that they will see him coming on the clouds of heaven. 'A greater than Solomon is here,' he claims. 'Heaven and earth shall pass away, my words never.' 'All things have been given me by my Father.' 'Before Abraham was, I am.' 'Come unto me, all ye who labour and are heavy laden.' The extraordinary thing is that, whereas on any other lips this quiet note of utter authority would have sounded like the presumption of a pathological delusion, on his lips such words ring credible and true. There is, moreover, the fact of his universality, and the incomparable spell he has laid on men and nations. No other leader or teacher or founder of a world faith ever thus bestrode the march of history, besieging the hearts of men and bridging the centuries. All our ordinary categories and measurements break down when applied to Jesus. He cannot be classified. In him a totally unprecedented factor has appeared on the scene. And if we agree that the emergence of such a personality is miraculous, must we not add that the resurrection fits into the pattern as the climax of the ministry and the attestation of a miracle which had been there all along? Therefore let no one be misled by the specious, shallow argument that to believe in the resurrection is to renounce or to defy reason. On the contrary. It is to see the whole of life in the light of a new coherent rationality.

Up to this point, I have been arguing that the scientific historian, even apart from faith, must feel the challenge of the evidence. Surely Professor C. F. D. Moule is not putting the matter too strongly when he declares: 'The birth and rapid rise of the Christian Church therefore *remain an unsolved enigma for any historian who refuses to take seriously the only explanation offered by the Church itself.*'[6]

III

But now comes the next step. For this has to be added: given faith, the evidence becomes convincing indeed, convincing to the point of being incontrovertible. 'Christian theology', writes Dr. Alan Richardson cogently, 'has never suggested that the "fact" of Christ's resurrection could be known apart from faith.'[7] And Bishop Lesslie Newbigin is even more emphatic: 'It has never at any time been possible to fit the resurrection of Jesus into any world view except a world view of which it is the basis.'[8]

Here it will be well to remind ourselves that if God is to be apprehended anywhere at all faith is absolutely vital. After all, who are we — on the basis of natural reason — to prescribe limits to what God can do, or to seek to eliminate the overtones of the transcendent from the Gospel story, as though the range of our experience could be the measuring-line of the purpose of God?

So let me put it like this. I may begin exploring the fact of Christ, intellectually and historically; but before I have gone very far I become aware that the fact is exploring me, spiritually and morally. I set out to search for the personality presented in the Gospels; and then, it may be gradually, it may be suddenly, I am conscious that the ultimate reality and heart of things is searching for me. I try to see what I can find in Christ, and God in Christ finds me. It is this divine self-authenticating element, this faith-creating quality, which makes the resurrection so finally compelling and convincing. It means that the resurrection is not simply something that can be located in an event and imprisoned in a past tense, an old story and a fading memory: it is present fact. As Emil Brunner has expressed it: 'You believe in the resurrection, not because it is reported by the apostles, but because the resurrected One himself encounters you, the living Mediator.'[9]

Just as faith sees, in the birth of Jesus, the eternal Word becoming flesh; in the life and ministry of Jesus, the Kingdom breaking through into time; in the atoning death of Jesus, God reconciling the world to himself — so now faith sees, in the resurrection of Jesus, God who created the universe and man at first bringing in a new creation and a new humanity. This is the intrinsic truth behind the apostle Peter's testimony on the day of Pentecost to the indestructibility of Jesus: 'It was not possible that he should be holden of death.'[10] The congruity of the resurrection with the person of Jesus and the purpose of God is manifest. This light no darkness could put out, for it was the authentic light of heaven. The resurrection is the mightiest of all the mighty acts of God.

Certainly this is the dominant emphasis of the New Testament. The men of the New Testament were not thinking about personal survival — they believed in that already. They were pointing to an act of God so stupendous that it was comparable only with what had happened at the first creation. 'The New Testament,' wrote Professor William Manson, 'throbs and rings with the sense that the line between expectation and fulfilment has been crossed.'[11] God raised up Jesus, not simply to give credence to man's immemorial hopes of life beyond the grave, but to shatter history and remake it by a cosmic, creative event, ushering in a new age and a new dimension of existence. In this event, focusing as it does the widsom and power and love of God, there lies for the world the potency of the redemption of history from meaninglessness and frustration, and for the individual the gift of life eternal in the midst of time and a blessed life hereafter.

For something has once for all gained a foothold on the darkened scene of history, something that transforms the outlook utterly. In and with the resurrection of Christ the whole world has been recreated. There has been released into this sphere of corruption and ruin and decay a force which really can make all things new. It is because Christ is risen, and men can be new creatures risen with him; it is because he has passed into the heavens, bearing all history on his heart, humanity's great High Priest and Intercessor; it is because, through the Holy Spirit, the same Jesus with whom the disciples walked in the days of his flesh, the same Lord whom the apostles knew and worshipped, is present with us now — because of this we can be sure that ultimately the hope of a new world is not illusory. It is a magnificent incontrovertible reality. The prospects are as bright as the promises of God, and the possibilities as illimitable as the victory of Christ.

It is this exciting New Testament emphasis we need to recapture today. It is a shame to take dully and as a matter of course, as we so often do, an event by which the whole human story has been turned inside out and refashioned, all the struggles of mankind suffused with the light of a deathless hope, and all our own weakness given the opportunity of being immediately linked up with Christ's all-conquering strength. His word to us is the same word which John of the Revelation heard: 'Fear not; I am the first and the last: I am he that liveth, and was dead; and, behold, I am alive for evermore.'[12] Christ is risen: let us rejoice!

J. S. STEWART

1 *To and Fro About the City.*

2 Romans 1:4.

3 Luke 16:31.

4 This is the meaning of 'Maranatha' in 1 Cor. 16:22, which is properly understood as a prayer, as in Rev. 22:20: See N.E.B.

5 Gal. 2: 20.

6 Moule, *The Phenomenon of the New Testament,* p.13 (Prof. Moule's italics).

7 Richardson, *History Sacred and Profane,* p.206.

8 Newbigin, *Honest Religion for Secular Man,* p.53.

9 Brunner, *I Believe in the Living God,* p.93.

10 Acts 2:24.

11 Manson, *Jesus and the Christian,* p.169.

12 Revelation 1:17, 18.

Doesn't the miraculous birth of Jesus give him an unfair advantage over us?

During the last war, when London was severely bombed, newspapers often showed photographs of the King and Queen visiting the bombed sites and talking to the people who had lost their homes. There's no doubt it did help to comfort people. They were grateful and felt encouraged by this personal concern shown by such important people. But others, looking at the photographs, felt angry. *'They* haven't lost their homes,' they said. 'The King and Queen have safe, deep shelters, and if Buckingham Palace did get bombed they would have plenty of other homes, just as luxurious. What use is their visit and their sympathy? They don't know what life is really like. Now if the King and Queen lived the way ordinary people do, that would mean something.'

You may or may not approve of monarchy, and you may or may not think the things royalty do are useful. But there is no doubt they do not share the hardships and chances of ordinary life (they may have others to bear, but that is not the point). And many people feel this way about Jesus. Maybe he was very kind and understanding, but it was really just royalty visiting the slums. He was the Son of God, he did not have to cope with our worries and muddles, our petty little feelings and our dreary little fears. He didn't need to watch out for himself, or worry about his future or his family. He may have suffered but it was an heroic kind of suffering, a great tragic drama. It wasn't like our sordid illnesses, worries about bills, our jealousies and envies and loneliness. He was all right, Jack.

It's natural people should think like this, because for centuries Christians very often used the image of royalty to give an idea of the glory and beauty and power of God. They spoke of the coming Jesus as if it had been a royal visit, an immense condescension for a time, before he returned to his proper state of splendour and majesty. And the fact that Jesus was God's Son was emphasized in this way, very strongly, especially because some people were saying that, after all, Jesus was just a man like anybody else, except that God had, as it were, 'taken him over' at his Baptism, and carried out his work of salvation through him. No, said the Church Councils, Jesus was not a puppet, he was a real man who was always God's Son — that was his own nature, not an extra.

Nowadays, this image of royalty, and the emphasis on Jesus being truly God's Son, has made a lot of people feel, Well, that's fine, but I'm not interested. If he was all that glorious and divine, he's got nothing to say to me, because I'm not. He can go slumming if he likes but I'm not queueing up for the hand-out!

And all this about the Virgin birth, nothing earthy like sex mixed up in it, it's altogether too good to be true; why couldn't he be born like us and *really* share our life? If he cares for us, he would.

The answer is that since he cares for us, he did, and the Virgin Birth is part of the way that caring is shown up.

It is true, of course, that the earliest Christians did not mention the Virgin Birth as far as we know. The Gospel writers who mention it wrote during the second half of the first century, when there were already flourishing groups or 'churches' of Christians round the Mediterranean. The interest in exactly *how* Jesus came to be what he was came late. It is the same thing as when two people meet and fall in love. At first all they care about is the marvellous fact that they are, and that they love each other. It is so miraculous and glorious that nothing else matters. But after a while they begin to want to know more about each other, about their families, childhood, home, and so on.

It was like that with the early Church. At first, just to know him, and his love, was enough. Then they began to wonder and ask about the background to Jesus's death and resurrection. They wanted to know what he said and did in his public life, what people thought about him, how he showed his power and explained his mission. They wanted to know what made him what he was. What was his background?

The writers of the different Gospels were all answering different kinds of questions about the 'background' to Jesus's work as Saviour. Matthew's Gospel is answering questions from Jewish Christians. They asked, Is Jesus really the Messiah that our people were waiting for? How did his life fulfil the Jewish prophecies? Mark's Gospel was probably put together in Rome, and like Matthew's it used stories and collections of sayings of Jesus that were already being circulated among the Churches. But the questions that Mark answered were different. The Christians in Rome wanted to know, mainly, what was he *like* as a person?

Luke was writing mainly for non-Jewish (Gentile) Christians. They weren't all that interested in Jewish prophecies, but they wanted to know, How was this Jewish man able to bring salvation to us, Gentiles? What was it that made him so special? And John's Gospel, written some time after the others, was quite different again, and seemed to be answering the questions of the whole Church, by then fairly well-established: How is God with us, now, in Jesus? If his life is over, what is he to us?

It is easy to see that writers who were asked such different questions would give different accounts of the same events, and would also pick out different events to record and comment on. And it isn't hard to guess which ones would be interested in the manner of Jesus's birth. It isn't important to Mark, who cares mainly about Jesus's character, as it is shown in his grown-up life and public work. It isn't important to John, who is showing Jesus' interest in all the world, in every man, now and always. But Matthew and Luke both have accounts of his birth, though for very different reasons.

Matthew's Gospel (never mind who wrote it, that argument is interesting but not important here) tells how a Messenger of God (the word 'angel' means 'messenger') told a Jew called Joseph that his young betrothed was pregnant because that was God's will. This child was to be, in a sense, the child of Israel's whole history, not just of one family. Joseph's family was descended from King David, the great King and hero. The Jews expected that the saviour whom the prophets had promised would come from David's family, the royal family of Israel. Matthew's Gospel is saying, He *did* come from David's family, but not simply because he happened to have a father who belonged to that clan. This boy is the child of God's promise, the One you have been waiting for, *the* child of Israel. In the Old Testament the prophets sometimes talk about Israel as the bride of God. God has chosen this people and loved them and made them his own — 'married' them to himself. The Messiah, the Christ, is the Son of God and of Israel. But Matthew's Gospel is saying, this boy, Jesus, wasn't simply sent down from Heaven in clouds of glory to drive out God's enemies, as many Jews expected. He was human, he was born of a human mother, into a real family, and a very ordinary one in spite of their royal ancestors. This Child fulfils the old prophecies, he really is the Son of David, he is the Lord's Anointed ('Christ' means 'anointed'), but he isn't what you expected. He is the child of an ordinary working man's family, and that is why so many of his people rejected him.

When one looks at it carefully, it is clear that Matthew's Gospel is telling us that what later was called the 'Virgin birth' is actually showing that Jesus is not an angel, or any heavenly being, but a man, a Jewish man. His conception arouses village gossip and worry and suspicion, and even Joseph needs a message from God to set his mind at rest about all the gossip, yet he *is* the one sent to 'save the people from their sins'.

The story of the conception and birth of Jesus in Luke's Gospel is the most familiar to us, from endless pictures of the Annunciation and Nativity, from plays, poems and hymns. Luke's purpose was different from Matthew's. He was writing for people who were accustomed to tales of gods wandering the earth in human form, testing people and helping them. They knew the stories of heroes whose father was a god but who had a human mother, and who therefore had divine gifts and powers. Luke's story of the conception and birth of Jesus is telling something quite different. The account of the message to Mary draws on stories in the Old Testament, in which God sent a child to a woman who was barren, in such a way as to make it clear that this child was God's gift, and set aside for his service. In particular the story of Hannah, Samuel's mother, provided the framework for Luke's account, and Hannah's song of thanksgiving provides many of the images or phrases that Luke used in Mary's 'Magnificat' of praise and thanks. For Luke, like Matthew, was showing that this was the child of God's promise, born because God willed it, and for no other reason. 'The power of the Most High shall overshadow you', says the Messenger, and this reminded people of the stories of how the Cloud of Glory overshadowed the Temple which Israel built, and was the sign of God's power and presence among them. Emmanuel, God-with-us. God among his people, but not just on a royal progress. Conceived by a village girl in an obscure corner of the country, born in poverty and not even in a proper home, unrecognized except by a few shepherds — and shepherds were usually regarded as a rascally, unreliable lot. This isn't in the least like the pagan legends, Luke is saying. This isn't a god in disguise, nor a half-divine hero born into a royal family. This is God's son, but he is a man, and not even an obviously important one. Poor, unknown, a workman in a very ordinary family. Later his neighbours wouldn't believe there could be anything special about him. 'We know his family, his mother and brothers and sisters are still living here. Who does he think he is?' they said.

Much later, it is true, Christians endlessly emphasized Jesus's title of glory and majesty — King of Kings and Lord of Lords. But that was *much* later, for reasons I mentioned earlier. What struck people in the early days — and often upset them — was not Jesus's glory but his lack of it. The Gospels show him tired, hungry, asking questions, feeling depressed, let down by his friends, abused by enemies, misunderstood, captured, publicly humiliated and finally killed. Some Christians were so scandalized by this kind of thing that they worked out a theory that Jesus of Nazareth was not *really* the Son of God, but God's Son simply used his body and wasn't there when it died. God's Son, they said, didn't really suffer fatigue, hunger, ignorance, let alone the humiliation of death. And he wasn't born, but entered into the body of Jesus at his Baptism. But the orthodox Christian tradition would have none of that. It may be odd, the Church kept on saying, it may seem mad and even incredible, but what the Gospels say, we still say: Jesus is the Son of God, but he is *really* a man, not a pretence or a ghost or a demi-god or an angel, or anything else you care to think up. He is a *man*.

Matthew's Gospel and Luke's Gospel both make this clear, and one way they do it, as I have shown, is by pointing up the Virgin birth of Jesus. Both accounts show Jesus as the child of ancient promise, not only for the Jews but for the whole human race, the One who is to come, the Saviour for whom the whole world has waited, the One who winds up all of history and starts it off on a new course. And this moment at which God blazes out into history is the moment when a particular human life happens. The great myth-heroes all exist in a timeless period, before history. The gods in human form have no date. But Jesus was born at a particular moment in history. People argue about the date of his birth as they argue about the birth dates of Julius Caesar or Shakespeare.

So far, then, we can see that, to the men who wrote the Gospels, and to those who read them, Jesus's birth of a virgin was evidence not of his remote, divine character, but of his human realness. But it is perhaps St. John, who never mentions the Virgin birth at all, who can best make sense of it for us and show that, far from taking Jesus out of the tough, sordid realities of life, it plunged him into them.

Everyone, even people who don't believe a word of it, know the great introductory passage of the Gospel of John. John uses a different image to describe how Jesus is of God. We are used to the phrase 'Son of God' so much that we forget it is an image.

The close relationship between a father and his son, the fact they are the same 'kind' yet not identical, the fact that a son owes his existence to his father, yet isn't just a 'part' of him, that a father recognizes something of 'himself' in his son — all these help to convey *some idea* of the relationship of Jesus to God, whom he called Father. But because we have used the phrase so often we sometimes cannot really 'hear' it. It doesn't mean much at all. It can even be a barrier to understanding, as I suggested at the beginning, when we feel that if Jesus is son of God then he is too silk-lined and exalted altogether, and no sort of help to us ordinary men and women.

So here is John using a different image altogether, and one which may be more helpful. He calls Jesus God's 'word' or 'utterance'. He thinks of God knowing himself, uttering himself, and that self-expression is itself the fullness of God's life. John struggles to find words to express this closeness — yet difference. The Word was *with* God and the Word *was* God. As John sees it, everything that happened, everything made, happened and was made *among* this self-expression of God, this utterance of his life; everything was made through him, without him nothing was made, in him was life — and this life was the light of men.

So John sees the Word as with God in everything and for ever, yet as being for *men*. And so this Word is spoken, not only in 'heaven' but among men. It is still God's utterance, God's very self, but the Word God speaks to men is a *man*. The only possible language for God to speak to men is the language of human life. John thinks of the human world as the *home* of the Word, the natural place for him to be, though in fact most people don't recognize him. He came to his own home and his own people would not accept him. But, accepted or not, recognized or not, there he was: the Word became human and lived among us. The usual translation of the phrase is 'the Word was made *flesh*' and while this was once accurate, it has changed its meaning and now seems to us to mean that God's Word simply 'put on' a human body, or flesh as an extra. But what John meant, as the original language makes clear, is that God's Word, God's 'self-expression' was *human*. He didn't just 'put on' a human body, he *became* human, and his name was Jesus. No one, John points out, has seen God — yet Jesus makes him known, because, as John explains through the mouth of Jesus, later in the Gospel — 'I am in the Father and the Father in me'.

Why? Why all this build-up in the long tragic, comic, extraordinary story of the Jews? Why this odd way of coming?

Why this fantastic life and death, this explosion of life that simply dissolves death and turns history upside down? John answers: in order to give to all men the same life which God meant them to have and which was Jesus's own by nature and right. When he smashed through the final failure of death he let into the world this new life, so powerful that it would catch up in its vitality all who heard and loved it. He gave them power to become children of God, says John's Gospel — this is, people living the same life as himself.

Whatever way we think of Jesus's birth, then, we cannot seriously suppose that it gives him an 'unfair advantage'. What it does is to make him fully, utterly and tragically human. He is one of us, not in order to show how kind he is but in order to give us the life which we are born to have, but dare not grasp.

In a letter, John tries once more to put it over, this notion that Jesus is real, human, available to us, not *in spite* of being God's Word, but *because* he is. Nobody else could be as human as this because no other man would *dare* to be as open, as available, as completely *ours*, as Jesus was, and is. Listen to his words tumbling over each other as he struggles to put it across, because it matters so much to him and to us, for this is what the 'Virgin birth' is all about; and notice that John uses both 'Word' and 'Life' as names for Jesus, who is God's Son *for us*, God's Word *to us*, *our* Life:

> Something which has existed from the beginning, that we have *heard,* and we have *seen* with our own eyes, that we have watched and *touched* with our hands:
>
> The Word who is life — this is what we are talking about. That life was made visible: we saw it and we are giving our testimony, telling you of the eternal life which was with the Father and has been made visible to us. What we have *seen* and *heard* we are telling you, so that you too may be in union with us, as we are in union with the Father and with his son Jesus Christ. We are writing this to make our own joy complete.

ROSEMARY HAUGHTON

If Jesus was God, who looked after the world while He was in Palestine?

A good question! One very like it was propounded by a wise and good Archbishop: 'What was happening to the rest of the universe during the period of our Lord's earthly life?'[1] A quick answer to the archbishop's conundrum would be:—'God was ruling the universe.' Heaven was not empty. God continued to rule and reign throughout the whole universe while Jesus was on the earth. But the present question is more subtle and more difficult. *'If Jesus was God,* who looked after the world while he was in Palestine?' Can there be another God to do the ruling for him? No. We cannot enter on the road to polytheism, the belief in several 'gods'.

In the New Testament, 'God' is a proper name. Therefore there is only one. But the Christian creeds speak of 'God the Father': 'God the Son': 'God the Holy Spirit'. They are, of course, careful to state that these are not separate, distinct gods, but One. We are face to face with the doctrine of the Trinity.

There are now two possibilities open to me in trying to answer the question. One is to write a book — and it would have to be a long book; the other is to write briefly; and, although this means using terms that are less precise than might otherwise be the case, I feel sure that you will read with satisfaction that I have chosen the second plan. ('Of making many books there is no end'.)

It is told of a small girl that she was constantly worried by this doctrine of the Trinity and quite unable to understand her mother's earnest explanations. In desperation, her mother said: 'I'm going to give you something that was written long ago by wise people; not that you will understand it now, but because some day it will help a little.' As a last resort she handed her a copy of the Athanasian creed. The girl read it through carefully three times. Gradually her tears dried up and she said, 'Why didn't you give me this long ago? *It makes everything perfectly clear.'* For myself, I shouldn't have put it in that way about the Athanasian creed; but for some this may be the appropriate attitude, because of the comfortable and measured words of personal conviction. Others fall back on human analogies; illustrations, as it were, from our own experience of this mystery of *many* being *one*. To take a small example — I remember once calling at General Eisenhower's headquarters ('Shellburst') in France in 1944 about a matter of the welfare of the Army. I was told — and it was a welcome reassurance — 'Whenever you come, the officer who happens to be on duty, British or American, will be able to answer your questions. There are a whole lot of us, but we all think the same way.' There was a tiny light thrown by these words on the mystery of the Incarnation; for God the Father and Christ the Son may be sundered in our thought, but they are one in the divine purpose for mankind. Another possibility is to think of our own faculties like the familiar three: Memory, Understanding, Will. They appear to be quite separate and yet they have the unity of our own person. Or we may think of an experience which comes to all of us, I trust, at some time; the sense that for once at least we have caught ourselves doing what is right and good. Some would go on to imagine that they have acquired merit: they have done something rather fine. But then, when they kneel to say their prayers, they realize that it was only through the goodness of God that they were able to act rightly. It was 'all of grace'. Here is a mystery on the level of our own life: All is of God, yet it came by our own responsible decision.

On the other hand, there is always a danger in taking a human illustration to illumine our thoughts of Christ's life and nature. *We* are sinners: *he* is Saviour. There is mystery here which our inadequate figures of speech may conceal rather than clarify.

The creeds have at least tried to make sure that we face up to the *real* mysteries and are not contented with premature, too easy solutions. The truth about God is not likely to be expressed without remainder in neat sentences and words of one syllable. Some have even said that it is not possible to say what God is like but only what he is *not*. Even wiser men have thought that the best way of thinking of God is to speak, not *about* him, but *to* him. In prayer comes a true understanding of God.

Statements of the Christian faith speak of God the Father, and of God the Son. It was also found inescapable to speak of God the Spirit. We can, fortunately, for this article, confine our inquiry to the four words, 'If Jesus was God . . . '

Look first at his own words and actions. He knew that the Father was still ruling in Heaven (Matthew 11:25.) He called for the Father's help in deeds of mercy. He knew the limitations of his earthly life. ('Of that day and hour', he said, 'knoweth no man, neither the Son but the Father.') (Mark 13:32). Most important of all, he spent many hours praying to the Father; and we may think specially of his communion with God in the Garden of Gethsemane, and his words from the Cross, 'Father, into thy hands I commend my spirit.' Already, then, it is possible for us to confirm the statements of the creeds on one point. It would be misleading to speak of Jesus as God – and to stop there. Jesus is *God the Son*. The mystery is lightened by this carefulness in words; for, if Jesus were all that there is of God, we should indeed have on our hands the puzzle concerning the control of the universe while he was on earth. It is true that God is also *our* Father, and we too are his sons. But in a very special way Jesus was recognised as *The* Son. We see this most clearly perhaps in the baptism in Jordan. The account of that inner experience must have come from the words of Jesus himself: he thought of himself as a very special Son. (Matthew 3:16–17.) (See also Luke 3:22.) He was truly man and also truly God.

Really and truly man. His powers were limited, physical and mental. He grew tired. He wept. And his knowledge was that of his own period. For him, the sun circled round the earth, though to-day we know that our world moves in an orbit round the sun. Even his moral insight seems to have grown and developed as it does with all men. Strangest of all, as it seems to some, he could be tempted. He was 'in all points tempted like as we are'. Yet without sin, we know; but the struggle was real; even, as we see from the account of his temptation (and it must have been his own account) agonizingly real, perhaps terrifyingly real.

Really and truly God. It is rather startling to find that one of the very earliest mistakes made about him was a heresy called 'docetism'. It denied that he was really a man. The early Christians had to contend for his true *humanity* against those who were so eager to proclaim him as more than man that they succeeded in making him seem to be not a real man at all, but just God in a disguise. In this connection I sometimes recall the soldier who wrote home that he was camped on the Mount of Olives; and received a reply from his dear grandmother reminding him that the Mount of Olives wasn't a real place: it was 'in the Bible' she said. So, even though they knew about the life of Christ in Palestine, his wanderings, his preaching, his healings, his death on the Cross; even perhaps when there were still those who could boast that their grandparents had seen him, there were some who denied that he was a real man, so convinced were they that he came from God's side.

From the Gospels we learn three things in particular by which men and women were impressed and solemnized. He is the Sinless One: he is the Saving One: he is the Reigning One. That is, he stands before us as *Perfect Man: Saviour of the World: Lord of all.*

1. *He is The Sinless One.* 'He was in all points tempted like as we are; yet without sin.' (Hebrews 4:15.) We have said that his temptations were real struggles. Was he really able to sin? — that question has vexed many generations. The answers seem to be in opposition and yet both to be true! He *was* able (or it would be no real temptation): yet he was *not able* (for at least we must say that God was with him, the Father with the Son). A helpful suggestion is that we ought to put it another way and say: he was *able not to sin:* such was the holiness of his being that sin and temptation were overwhelmed by it.

2. *He is The Saving One.* He had power over nature and over disease — a power, it is true, that was always dependent on his oneness with the Father. Above all, he had the power, and he claimed the right, to forgive sins. He saves — and only God can do that. The scribes and Pharisees were quite right in saying that this claim to forgive sins and save men and women was a claim to be more than a man. Jesus was indeed proclaiming that he was in a special way the Son of God. Moreover, only One who is eternal can save; so that we are compelled to give to him a timeless background: he belongs to eternity: he existed before he came into this world.

3. *The Risen and Reigning One.* He lived before his life on earth. Similarly we are bound to say that he lives on now when his earthly life is over. He is the Risen and Reigning One. The name which the first Christians gave to him was that of *Lord.* The Greek word (Kyrios) stands for the Hebrew name of God in the Old Testament (Yahweh, or Jehovah) which was too holy to be pronounced. Rightly, therefore, we worship him: rightly we pray to him or in his name: rightly we call him Lord. He was from the beginning of time, and he reigns now for evermore. On earth he was truly God — God in human form, God the Son.

Quite clearly he was a man; and quite clearly he was more than man. Some people try to argue that Jesus, though a good man, even a sinless man, is 'just like one of us.' The complete answer lies in asking, 'Like *which* one of us?' Our hearts condemn us; but from the lips of Jesus there came no words of confession, no prayer that he might be forgiven. He alone, of all who ever lived on earth, had nothing to confess, no need to be forgiven.

There have been many earnest attempts to show how it is that he can be both God and man. Some of them have been rightly rejected by the Christian Church. One of these would say that Jesus, because of his sinless life and devotion and obedience, was raised to a place of glory, promoted, as it were, to the realm of the divine. Another proclaimed that he was God all the time, but chose to wear the guise of humanity. A third theory sought to take a middle position and ended by making out that Jesus was neither fully human nor fully divine, but something of each, a kind of Grecian demi-god, not the Christian Redeemer.

The second chapter of Philippians and the opening verses of John's Gospel offer profound ways of seeking to illuminate this mystery; and it would be true, I think, to say that many other sincere theories have a rightful place, if each is presenting a facet of the truth. Because none is adequate, or ever can be, each must in its measure be untrue; yet, while each alone is in error, together they may serve the truth. Nevertheless, the truth is vaster than any theory of it and transcends all theories put together.

What happened at the Incarnation, when Jesus became man, entering our world as a child? Paul, in Philippians, chapter 2, speaks of Christ humbling himself. The Greek word speaks of a 'self-emptying'. He surrendered his divine omnipotence, his omniscience, his omnipresence, in order that he might become a man among men, with all the limitations that are implied in manhood.

The doctrine of the Trinity is nowhere defined in the New Testament; but the evidence for it is there. Jesus often spoke of the Father in Heaven, and he tells of the Comforter who is to come; but time and thought and Christian experience were all needed before the young Church could grasp the full meaning of what had happened. Fortunately for us, behind the doctrine lie many 'infallible proofs' (to use some words from the beginning of the Book of Acts.) Three times St. Luke tells of mysterious appearances of Jesus: the first was at the Transfiguration; the second on the Road to Emmaus (these two are recorded in his Gospel); the third is described in Luke's second book, the Acts of the Apostles. Each time he gives only the theme of the discourse, when we might greatly desire to know the actual words of Jesus. There was, inevitably, much that could not be expressed in words. The highest cannot be spoken. (Perhaps that is the origin of all great music. The poet Sidney Lanier says that 'Music is love in search of a word'.) There are thoughts too lofty to go into the narrow framework of speech. Of the main attempts to reduce the doctrine of the Trinity to the medium of words, two of the most famous are classed as 'heresies', a word which originally meant no more than individual choices, but then came to signify sects, or opinions which were actually contrary to the orthodox Christian belief. One of these holds that Jesus is only a mode of the divine being — so doing less than justice to the independence of Jesus as a real person. The other implies that the persons of the Trinity are united after a fashion whose nearest human parallel is that of a family or college or nation or commonwealth — a theory which falls far short of proclaiming the perfect unity of will that exists between the divine persons. Confining ourselves, as promised, to the relation between the Son and the Father, we find much illumination once more in the prayers of Jesus. His mind was often hidden even from the twelve disciples. They were not yet able to understand. Now and then there might come a flash of light and they could guess something of what was happening within his heart. One day, for example, he cried out, in unexpected severity and anger, against the Pharisees: and they saw how he had long been pondering on this bitter tragedy, of a people misled by their leaders. Another day, as the road wound round the corner of a hill, they came suddenly in sight of the city of Jerusalem. To their astonishment, when Jesus looked down on it, he burst into tears. With a flash of understanding they saw how much he loved the place, and how much he mourned over its cruel obstinacy. But the real, deep insight came to them when Jesus prayed. It is the same writer, Luke, who alone mentions the prayer of Jesus at his baptism. The circumstances are full of meaning. It is the first appearance of Jesus after the silent years, the days spent in obscurity so that we have no record of them except for the single glimpse of him in the Temple at the age of twelve. Appropriately, the first account of his return to the world speaks of his prayer; and we wonder how often and how earnestly he must have prayed in the long interval of time. It was because of this, no doubt, that John the Baptist recognized him as one who was quite different from the other listeners. This bold prophet, who could denounce Pharisees and rebuke kings, sets aside all his lofty bearing in *this* Presence. He has baptized many; has seen men of all kinds, and seen through them; but hitherto no one like this had come to seek baptism. Others have all bowed before this greatest prophet; but before this Man there bows down the sinner in the prophet. We have recognized that there is a special mystery about the prayers of Jesus. If, as we believe, he was no less than God, how could God pray to God, or what need could he have that was not already granted by God? It may help us to understand this if we realize that prayer is not simply *asking*. Jesus *did* pray about his own needs. (In Gethsemane he prayed earnestly about the suffering he was soon to endure.) He prayed for his disciples (John 17:6 ff.) He prayed for Peter by name (Luke 22:32.) He prayed for his enemies when they were nailing him to the Cross (Luke 23:34). But, again and again, his prayer was not to ask anything, but simply to have communion with God. It is sometimes said that strong men do not need to pray: they take what they want. Jesus at all events felt the necessity. He was sinless; yet he could not go on without prayer. 'What a commentary on *our* need of it!' So someone has written, adding, 'If he needed it, being what he was, how must we need it, being what we are.'

There were, we can be sure, many people who believed in him because of his miracles. They wanted signs, and here they had them in plenty. But that, in fact, is not what he desired. He is to be his own credential. No argument can compel belief in Christ by dwelling on his miracles, or on the special manner in which he entered this world or departed from it. Only belief in his Person could convert. And that is revealed, not alone in the accounts of his life on earth, but also in his communion with his Father — and also, as we ought at once to add, in our communion with him in our worship, alone or in Church.

One final suggestion I wish to make. We saw how it has been said that Jesus, in coming to live in Palestine, put off the divine attributes, 'emptying' his nature of omnipotence, omniscience, omnipresence, so that he might live as man among men, circumscribed by all the limitations implied in humanity. There is, I believe, something much more important to be noticed here. The chief divine attribute, that which supremely makes God to be God, is not infinite power, nor infinite knowledge, nor ubiquity: it is *Love*. There was immeasurable sacrifice in the Love of God the Father which 'sent his Son' into the world: in all that the Son was to suffer, God too suffered: Love is infinitely vulnerable. And there was immeasurable sacrifice in the Love which brought Jesus to the earth, in full knowledge of what was involved. In becoming man he laid himself open to man's temptations; and he offered himself a willing victim of scorn and contempt, of intrigue, betrayal, pain and death. As a real man, he displayed perfect holiness and perfect Love in the confines of perfect humanity. To understand something of this perfect and holy Love is to see how the ruling of the universe was not set at risk by his coming. On the contrary, when this divine and holy atoning Love of Jesus was brought to bear, a new creative power was revealed and released. Thus it would be truer to say that the ruling of the universe was not abandoned, nor left in the hand of God the Father alone, but was shared. The fulness of Time was come, when mankind knew that they could receive redemption through One who had lived their life victoriously: One who was manifest as God the Son, sent forth by the Father, raised by the Father from the grave, and at last received again by the Father when his redemptive mission was fulfilled.

When we read the first chapter of John's Gospel we can speak, quite naturally, of Jesus as the 'Creative Word'; the agent and medium of creation. 'All things were made by him; and without him was not any thing made that was made.' This Gospel might be called 'The Second Book of Genesis'; telling of the time when a new creation came into being, when God spoke over the darkness of the world, saying, 'Let there be light'; and there was light — in the face of Jesus Christ, his own Son.

The archbishop wondered how the universe could run if this Creative Word, this agent and medium of creation, were now alive as a man in Palestine. My answer would be simply this:— Redemption is the *re*-creation of the universe. It restores man to his real self, one who was made in the image of God. Jesus, by his life and sacrifice, brought about the redemption of a fallen world; the rebuilding of a broken universe. *In a new sense* we behold him, on earth, the Creative Word, the agent and medium of Creation.

It has been said that 'he reigns from the Cross'. These are not just the words of poetical adoration. He is the world's Redeemer who rules and reigns as Lord of all.

E. P. DICKIE

1 William Temple, *Christus Veritas*, p. 142.

If Christ had to die 'to redeem the world', why blame Pilate?

In life there is more than one kind of *must*. There is the *must* of complete and absolute physical necessity. If a man falls over a precipice he *must* fall. He has no choice in this. Short of suspending or abrogating the laws by which the physical world continues to exist, he *must* fall. On the other hand there is the *must* of moral choice. When John Bunyan was considering the cost of remaining loyal to what he believed to be right, he said that he felt like a man who was pulling down his house on the top of his wife and children. Yet, he said, he kept thinking: 'I *must* do it! I *must* do it!' That kind of *must* is quite different. The falling man *must* fall, and nothing that he can do can stop the fall. Bunyan *must* make and keep his decision, yet from the point of view of possibility he could easily do otherwise. He did not need to go on; he could quite easily have turned back from his self-chosen path. So, then, we must begin by being clear that there is a *must* of physical necessity, from which a man has no possible escape, and there is a *must* of moral necessity, from which, if a man chooses to do so, it is perfectly possible to escape.

Now Jesus uses the word *must* of the future which lay ahead of him:

> And he began to teach them that the Son of Man *must* suffer many things, and be rejected by the elders and the chief priests and the scribes, and be killed, and after three days rise again (Mark 8:31).

But he also says:

> I lay down my life that I may take it again. No one takes it from me, but I lay it down of my own accord (John 10:18).

It is thus clear that, when Jesus used the word *must*, he was not thinking in terms of an inescapable physical necessity, but of what was for him a self-chosen, completely voluntary, morally chosen necessity. Jesus was not driven by a fate outside his control. God set before him the goal, but he was directed towards it by the compulsion of his own choice. That Jesus could have turned away from his task there is no possible doubt. If ever there was a real struggle in this world, that struggle took place in the Garden of Gethsemane (Mark 14:32–41), and that struggle was between the desire to turn back and the *must* of going forward.

We must now ask: What was the task that Jesus must do? Different answers may be given to that question, but they will all issue in the same goal. The task of Jesus was to bring God to men and to bring men to God. He had to take away the barrier between men and God. He had to turn the estrangement into nearness, the hostility into friendship, the enmity into love, the fear into trust. His task was the task of reconciliation. But the reconciliation was the reconciliation of men. God did not need to be reconciled to men. God's attitude had never been anything else but love. It was because God so loved the world that he sent Jesus at all (John 3:16). It was the attitude of men, not of God, which had to be changed. It was with the offer and the appeal of God that Jesus came.

As John had it: 'The Word became flesh' (John 1:14). The Greek for *word* is *logos*. *Logos* does mean *word*. A word is a means of communication, and this will mean that Jesus is God's communication to men. But *logos* also means *mind* or *reason*, and a word is the expression of a thought. So, if Jesus is the *logos* he is the expression of the thought of God. In him the mind of God becomes a person. In him the attitude of God is fully and perfectly displayed.

What is that attitude? What is the mind of God? When we see Jesus healing the sick, comforting the sad, feeding the hungry, offering friendship to the outcast and the sinner and to the people with whom no respectable person would have anything to do, we can say: 'This is the attitude of God to men. This is how God feels towards men.' This is to say that Jesus confronts men with the love of God.

But when men were thus confronted, what happened? They rejected Jesus, because they loved their own laws and their own systems and their own conventions more than they loved God. But if men would not answer to the love of God, this did not stop Jesus loving them. The whole life of Jesus is God saying to men: 'You can insult me, you can forsake me, you can ill-treat me, you can be disloyal to me, I will not stop loving you.' That is why Jesus had to die: he had to die to show that there were no lengths to which the love of God was not prepared to go. If Jesus had not died, there would have been some point at which, so to speak, the love of God said: 'Thus far and no farther.' But he loved men to the end (John 13:1). He showed the complete indestructibility, the complete limitlessness of the love of God. Nothing that men could do, not even if they killed him, would stop that love. This is why he had to die, and this is what his death proves and reveals about God.

Confronted with that love, men destroyed Jesus. In one sense they had to. They had to eliminate him, if they were to keep their own way of life, their own way of thought, their own idea of religion. But this is not the *must* of absolute necessity; this again is the *must* of a self-chosen way. It was because of their own choice that men killed Jesus, not because of an inescapable necessity. This was the reaction of humanity confronted with the offer and the demand of the love of God.

It was the *must* of love which brought Jesus to the cross, and love cannot ever be anything but spontaneous; it was not the *must* of absolute necessity. It was the *must* of self-will that made men kill Jesus; it also was not the *must* of absolute necessity.

And now we come to Pilate. Palestine was under the government of the Romans, and, while the Romans left the Jews a large amount of self-government, the Jews did not have the right to carry out the death sentence. Sentence of death had to be passed by the Roman governor and carried out by the Roman military authorities. So then, the Jews could try Jesus according to their own law, and they could decide that he was guilty of a crime deserving death, but it was with Pilate that the last word lay. It is then necessary to look at Pilate.

Pilate must have had an excellent military and administrative career or he would never have been put in charge of so difficult a district as Palestine. In point of fact, Palestine was not itself a full province; it was part of the province of Syria, and the governor of Syria was Pilate's superior officer.

Pilate was in charge of Judaea from A.D.26 to 36, and the trouble was that the wisdom he must have had to arrive at that post at all seemed to leave him entirely. He made three almost incredible mistakes.

The first occasion was shortly after his arrival. Jerusalem was not the administrative headquarters of the Roman governor; his headquarters was in Caesarea, which was very largely a Gentile city. When there were large crowds in Jerusalem, as, for instance, at the Passover time, Roman troops were drafted into Jerusalem to deal with any possible disturbance. The standards of a Roman regiment were not flags; they were poles with a little metal image of the reigning Roman emperor on the top of them. The Roman emperor was officially a god; the image of the emperor was therefore to the Jews an idol and a graven image, and all previous governors had, in deference to the principles of the Jews, removed the images from the standards before troops were marched into Jerusalem. Pilate refused to do so. The Jews neither used nor threatened violence. They besought him to have the images removed. Pilate refused. A large deputation of the Jews came down to Caesarea and for five days entreated him to respect their religion. At last he assembled them in an open place on the pretext of being about to give his decision. He suddenly surrounded them with armed troops, and threatened that, if they did not stop their entreaties, they would there and then be massacred. The Jews simply bared their necks, and bade the soldiers kill. Not even Pilate could contemplate such a cold-blooded massacre, and he had to give in. It was a disastrous beginning for any governor to make.

Pilate never seemed to learn how to deal with Jews. He wished to bring a new water-supply into Jerusalem, which indeed the city badly needed. He proposed to finance the scheme by raiding the Temple treasury. The people protested violently. Pilate distributed his troops, dressed in ordinary civilian clothes, in disguise through the streets. They were armed with clubs. Pilate made another appeal to the Jews to disperse. They refused. At a given signal the troops fell on the crowds. Death and massacre were not in Pilate's mind; he merely wanted to clear the streets, but the troops got out of hand and savagely attacked the Jewish crowds and many died that night. A Roman province could report its governor for misconduct, and now that threat hung over Pilate's head.

His third error of judgment seems slight, but it had serious consequences. In Herod's palace Pilate dedicated certain gilt votive shields to the honour of Tiberius the Roman emperor. There was no image on the shields, only the emperor's name. But the emperor was a god; the shields were a kind of prayer for his health; and the Jews could not bear it. When Pilate refused to remove the shields, the Jews appealed to Tiberius; and Tiberius took the part of the Jews and sent orders that the shields should at once be removed. Pilate now knew that the emperor was well aware that there was trouble in Judaea, and that he must walk carefully.

The Jews had Pilate just where they wanted him. They could blackmail him with threats of report to the emperor, and on his record in Judaea, Pilate stood a very good chance of losing his

province, if such a report reached Rome. This is precisely what
the Jews did twice over. When the Jewish court examined Jesus
to find out what charge could be levelled against him, the result
of the investigation was a charge of blasphemy (Luke 22:70, 71).
But that is not the charge on which they brought him to Pilate.
The charge they made to Pilate was: 'We found this man
perverting our nation, and forbidding us to give tribute to Caesar,
and saying that he himself is Christ, a king' (Luke 23:2). The
Jews knew the charge was false; Pilate knew the charge was false.
But it was a charge on which Pilate was bound to proceed. He
could have laughed a charge of blasphemy out of court, and no
doubt would have done so. He dared not seem to be indifferent
to a charge of political sedition. And the Jews rubbed in another
exercise in blackmail. 'If you release this man,' they said, 'you are
not Caesar's friend; everyone who makes himself a king sets
himself against Caesar' (John 19:12). They could not have said
more plainly that a report was going to Rome unless Pilate gave
them their way with Jesus.

Here then is the state of Pilate. He had to choose between
giving justice to Jesus and the high probability of losing his
province. He had got himself into a position when he *must*
condemn Jesus in order to save himself. He must throw Jesus to
the wolves or face consequences disastrous to himself and to his
career.

Here we are back again at the *must* and the *had to*. Pilate *must*
condemn Jesus. He *must* hand him over to the Jews to do with
him as they willed. But quite clearly there is no physical and
absolute necessity here. It was in one sense impossible for Pilate
to resist the Jews; it was in another sense perfectly possible for
him to defy the Jews to do their worst.

We have looked at Jesus and we have looked at Pilate. Now we
must look at the great basic question which underlies this whole
matter. Just what is the relation of the will of God and the will of
man? To put the question in its usual terms, has man got
free-will, or is everything fated or predestined? We can come at
the answer to this in two ways.

First, it is inconceivable that God's will would compel a man
to commit a sin. God would simply cease to be God, if he was the
author of sin. God would no longer be the God of holiness and
love, if he was the originator of evil. This we must accept as a first
principle.

Second, if two things are to exist in the world at all, free-will is
a necessity. *Goodness* cannot exist without free-will. Before

goodness can exist there must be the possibility of free choice between two alternative courses of action. If a man is inexorably compelled to do something, he cannot be blamed for doing it. Blame can only arise when a man could have done otherwise. Goodness and free-will are inseparably linked to each other. *Love* cannot exist without free-will. Of all things in this world, love must be spontaneous. There is no such thing as a coerced love. Love must be the free response of one person to another. So then without free-will neither goodness nor love can exist. How it happened we cannot tell, but if God wished men to be in a relationship of obedience and love to himself, then he had to begin by making men free.

This is not to say that life is purposeless, nor is it to say that God has left men entirely to themselves. There is nothing that a man is *compelled* to do; there is much that he is *meant* to do. When we are thinking of the relationship between God and man, it is always legitimate to use the analogy of the relationship between parent and child. A parent has hopes, and plans, and dreams, and prayers for his child, but he cannot compel the child to fulfil them. That lies with the child. A parent can in his mind plan a child's career, but he cannot compel the child either to accept or to carry out the plan. It is so with man and God. God has a purpose for every man, but not even God can compel a man to accept that purpose — and that purpose can never be that the man should do evil and commit sin.

But if a man has this freedom as far as God is concerned, how does he get himself entangled in the constricting *musts*? How in the end was Pilate compelled to consent to the crucifixion of Jesus? There are three things which can be said.

First, *a man is at the mercy of his values.* A man's action will be dictated by that which he believes to be valuable. Now values are something which a man chooses, and which in the end become an in-built part of him. He may begin by thinking and assessing values; bit by bit his reaction becomes automatic as the value becomes part of himself. To take a simple example, if a man's highest value is money, he will not be particular as to how he gets it, or as to whom he crushes in the process. The poverty and want of others will mean nothing to him. It is clear that Pilate's supreme value was career-ambition. He had to give in to the Jews and condemn Jesus or lose his job. He chose his job. And he did so because he had made himself like that by choosing certain values in life, until they were in-built into his character.

Second, *a man is at the mercy of his previous life.* If a man has done certain things, there are certain other things that he cannot do. A man's previous life either opens or shuts doors to him in the present. Pilate's previous conduct had made him an easy victim of Jewish moral blackmail. He was not in any position to say No.

Third, *a man is what he is by means of his previous decisions.* The progress of sin is a terrifying process. No man sins easily for the first time. He has a hesitation, a shudder, a sense of wrong when he does a wrong thing for the first time. He does it. He does it a second and third time, and each time it becomes easier to do. The hesitation vanishes, the shudder is stilled, the sense of wrong is dulled and desensitised. He goes on doing the thing, and the final stage comes when he cannot stop doing it. He is in its grip. Not only does he no longer want to say No; he cannot say No. In all probability Pilate had been running away from decisions for so long that he was incapable of making one.

From all this one inescapable conclusion emerges — *the only person who can destroy a man's free-will is himself.* He can make himself such that he cannot decide for the right. And that is what Pilate had done.

It is true that Jesus came into the world to follow a way that could end only in death. It was the spirit of the world which killed him. But the men who brought about his death, Pilate and all the rest of them, can never escape blame. God had not taken away their freedom. They had made themselves such that, when God appeared to them, they could do nothing but hate him. God did not make them like that; they made themselves like that.

WILLIAM BARCLAY

Why should we *be blamed or held responsible for the betrayal and crucifixion of Jesus?*

Why indeed? We are no more to be blamed or held responsible for the crucifixion of Jesus than for the assassination of Julius Caesar or the burning of Joan of Arc. If the words of the question be taken in their simple, normal, natural sense, there is no more that need be said.

But Christians like scientists and others of specialist learning are always apt to use a sort of shorthand or private language of their own which has to be learnt before their meaning can be understood, and it is well worth our while to enquire what is *meant* when it is said that we are to be blamed or held responsible for the crucifixion of Jesus.

In the first place, who are the 'we' that should be blamed or held responsible? If a schoolboy said to me, 'We won all our matches last term', I should not take that to mean necessarily that he was himself a member of the team. As a Briton I can thankfully say, 'We smashed the power of Napoleon; we emancipated the slaves; we won the Battle of Britain.' I can say that meaningfully though I personally made no contribution to any of these events. But I ought also to add, not thankfully at all, 'We burnt scores of poor women as witches; we made a pile of money out of the slave-trade, and we made war on China to force opium upon them', for the same 'we' did those things too. Or we could take the 'we' in the widest sense of the human race; *we* learnt how to kindle fire, to sow crops, to breed animals; we invented the wheel, the steam-engine, the aeroplane. Yes and from the beginning of history *we* have been at war with one another; we have been guilty of unimaginable cruelties to one another; millions have been slaughtered, millions have been enslaved.

> Force rules the world still,
> Has ruled it, shall rule it.
> Meekness is weakness.
> Might is triumphant.

Over the whole earth
Still it is Thor's day.

In this limited and impersonal sense 'we' are certainly responsible for the crucifixion of Jesus.

But the accusation comes nearer home than that. We are apt to think of the crucifixion of Jesus as an unique event in human history. Not at all! It was a typical event. *He* was unique; no one ever was so completely unselfish, so all-embracing in his compassion — especially for the needy, the sinners and the outcasts of society, so wholly 'the man for others' as was he; and he suffered the fate that might have been antecedently expected. Centuries before Christ came, the philosopher Plato had predicted that if ever the truly just man appeared upon earth, he would be crucified. Many have shared more or less in the character of Jesus. Bonhoeffer was hanged; Martin Luther King was shot; no man knows how many Christlike characters have died in concentration camps and gas chambers in modern times; how many, who have caught something of the spirit of Jesus, are rotting or tortured as political prisoners in many parts of the world today! This is the world in which we live. Can we claim that no blame and no responsibility for it rests on us?

But I think the accusation comes still nearer home. We all know that Judas Iscariot betrayed Jesus for money, and I suspect that it is precisely this which many of us have also done. Jesus said, 'Inasmuch as ye have done it unto one of the least of these my brethren, ye have done it to me'. Suppose, to take a simple instance, I have a cottage to let which is desperately needed by a homeless family, and suppose I insist upon so high (though perhaps intrinsically reasonable) a rent that the family will not really be able to afford enough coal to keep warm or enough food to eat; have I not betrayed Jesus for money just as Judas did? I cannot but think that in our competitive, capitalist system of society, Jesus is constantly being betrayed for money, and few of us can feel quite innocent.

But did not Peter also betray Jesus when he denied him? Betrayal is disloyalty. He denied him because there might have been very unpleasant consequences for himself if he had admitted that he was a disciple of this arrested Galilean. Do we suppose that we should have been more brave? If a small boy is being bullied at school, and I, a Christian, do nothing about it because of the probable unpleasant consequences to me personally, have I not done precisely what Peter did? Does not Jesus clearly say,

'Inasmuch as ye did it not unto that little boy, ye did it not unto me'? The situation is the same, though often less obvious, in the larger world. How unwilling we are to be unpopular for Jesus! Am I making myself an intolerable nuisance to the town council where I live till they do something, and do it quickly, for those who have no homes in which to live? Have I remembered that Jesus has identified himself with the stranger in our midst, the coloured man, the immigrant, with the underprivileged boys and girls who have no playground? I suspect that we have denied and betrayed Jesus again and again at cocktail parties and in the gossip of tea-parties, because we have not said for our neighbours what he would undoubtedly have said.

This brings me to my last point. There is much that is very obscure about the last days of Jesus on earth. I used to think that even if the crowds that used to hear him gladly did not suddenly change their minds and cry 'crucify him!', at least they were apathetic and could not be bothered to organize a counter-demonstration; but I think now that the arrest, the trial, the condemnation was a hole-and-corner affair, and that most people could not know what was happening till it was too late. At least it is plain that those primarily responsible for his crucifixion were the Sadducees and Pharisees (or most of them). The Sadducees were a worldly, wealthy party who controlled the temple and its finances; they represented the nearest approach in that day to what we call 'big business'. Now Jesus single-handed (though not, presumably, without popular support) by the sheer force of his personality and his blazing, holy anger had overturned the tables of the bankers and cleared the cattle-market out of the temple courts, quoting the Scriptures, 'My house shall be called a house of prayer for all nations'. That, said the Sadducees, is revolution; what is going to happen to our economic system and to our incomes? At all costs this fellow must be destroyed!

The Sadducees were worldly men; the Pharisees were good and religious men. Ever since, years before, Nehemiah had rebuilt the walls round the devasted city of Jerusalem the Jews had largely forgotten the universal religious teaching of their great prophets; they had turned in upon themselves; they regarded obedience to the letter of the Law as their first duty to God, and the more general precepts of the Law had been elaborated into a ceremonial system that covered every aspect and almost every activity of life. The Pharisees were very religious and utterly devoted, single-minded in their glad obedience to the Law. They despised the 'lesser breeds;' they had angry contempt for the ordinary people who did not, and could not, keep all the minute regulations now regarded as part of the Law. That is why, when Jesus said, 'How hardly shall they that have riches enter the kingdom of heaven', the disciples asked, 'Who then *can* be saved?', for you *had* to be a man of leisure and means to obey all the rules and regulations of religion. Jesus as with a sharp knife had cut through all these pettifogging regulations; the Sabbath was made for man, not man to keep the rules of the Sabbath; it is justice and mercy that God requires, not a servile obedience to man-made rules. Moreover he had gone out of his way to make friends with the publicans (the Quislings of their day) and the 'sinners', that is, those who did not and could not fulfil the details of the Law, 'outsiders' as we might call them; he had not even limited his mercy to those who were strict Jews; worst of all, perhaps, he had actually polluted himself by *touching* a leper that he might heal him. This, said the Pharisees, is revolution; it is turning our whole religious tradition upside down; at all costs this fellow must be destroyed.

Jesus was condemned by Pilate on a trumped-up political charge, but it was as a religious revolutionary that the authorities were determined on his death. All that was long ago. What is the sense of suggesting that *we* are responsible for the crucifixion?

It is not far-fetched to say that the Sadducees and Pharisees represented between them the established order of their day. Is the established order of our day so different that Jesus need not be any more rejected and destroyed as a revolutionary? Of course, in many ways it is *very* different. That old world has passed away. But what would Jesus say to *our* established order, and could our Establishment, as we call it, endure him any better than the Establishment of his own day?

It is not given to me to answer this question, but it is for all to ponder it. Jesus did not concern himself with politics, and he would not give us *political* answers to our problems today. But in two regards he gave insufferable offence to the Establishment of his day; he went out of his way to make friends with 'publicans and sinners', and in respect of religion he said that nothing was of any significance compared with love and mercy. We may say very confidently that today the coloured people would be his peculiar care. We could name many countries today where he would certainly be in prison if he were allowed to live. Again, he would, I am sure, be much more lenient in his judgment of many of our bankers and business men and Trade Unionists than are their political opponents, but he would make us see that our whole industrial and fiscal system is radically unjust, and that gradualness in reform is another name for delay. His teaching would be seen to be revolutionary. The police would attend his meetings, and a kindly judge might recommend him for psychiatric treatment. Is this too fanciful? He would be perhaps praised but certainly rejected by our political Establishment. And if he went on to speak of our expenditure on armaments and our duty to the less privileged peoples, he would surely be called a Communist here just as in Communist countries he would be condemned and silenced as a liberal or deviationist.

It is plain from the records that Jesus was a man of astonishing personal force; you could not overlook him, and you could not silence him. Suppose for a moment that someone with a force of personality and of character in any way comparable to that of Jesus were to put himself at the head of the movement we call 'student unrest', what would *The Times* say of him, or the I.T.V., or the leaders of our political parties? We are one of the few countries without a secret police and without the habit of assassination, but if such a person did to our economic order anything comparable to the cleansing of the temple two thousand years ago, he would, I suspect, be allowed to live — under supervision in a mental home. All the established forces of law and order would undoubtedly reject his teaching as 'impractical' and 'idealistic', and in truth it is in fact quite impractical unless one is prepared to put it into practice.

The political establishment would certainly reject him; would the religious establishment accept him? It has been said that the Old Testament is the long story of the Jews' disobedience to their God. A very large part of the history of Christianity is the story of the Church's disloyalty to Christ. Would he not today, seeing the enormous accumulated wealth of the churches say, 'sell all that thou hast and give to the poor'? Would he not say to the churches much what he said to the Pharisees long ago — 'you have made religion a matter of church-going and of a negative morality, thanking God that you are not as these beatniks or these women on the streets?'

> Rather will God be found,
> As once he was, 'midst scenes of crime and woe,
> In market-place, on execution ground,
> Or where poor travellers go
> Unarmed to Jericho,
> And missed of them that loiter in the aisle
> And from the oppressive world escape awhile.

There is temptation to be unfair and rhetorical about all this. Long ago it was said that 'the common people heard him gladly', and as individuals I would willingly believe that we also hear him gladly. But in respect of our political, industrial and economic ordering of society, in respect of our Defence policies or the attitude of the 'haves' to the 'have-nots' in our society, of the white race to the coloured races, of the respectable to the prostitutes and the drug-addicts and the 'outsiders' his word is revolutionary and utterly unacceptable. We did not betray and crucify Jesus, but those who did were just like us.

I cannot willingly bring myself to end upon this note, though I have answered my question as best I could. I said at the beginning that, as the insignificant new boy may say with pride, 'We won all our matches this term', so we may say, 'We learnt to kindle fire, to create the plough, the steam-engine, the aeroplane; we conquered at Trafalgar and won the Battle of Britain'. This we may say partly because we all belong together, and partly because in admiration and desire we identify ourselves with those who accomplished these feats for us. What man has done, we have done because we are all of a single human fellowship. In William Wilberforce we abolished slavery. Therefore also in Christ we have triumphed over the world and over sin. If with shame and contrititon we must say that 'we have crucified the Lord of glory', we may say also by faith and by desire that 'we have risen with Christ'; by love and by desire and under the all-enfolding Mercy the revolution has begun in us, and it shall yet appear in all the world when Jesus 'shall see of the travail of his soul and shall be satisfied'.

NATHANIEL MICKLEM

Why should a God of love allow his Son to die on a cross?

Why was the Cross necessary: why was there a Cross?

If we are to be orthodox, nothing is more certain than that God allowed the Cross. He let it happen. He used it. It is what upsets many young people today: this necessity of a Cross. 'Why should a God of Love allow his well-beloved Son — of all people — to die on a Cross?' is the secret question of many a soul. It so upsets them that they refuse to consider it. They feel God can never have meant it, and so — to escape their problem — they create in their mind the picture of a God of Love unable to prevent it: powerless in the face of man's sin. They cannot see God 'behind' the Cross, so they visualize it as all happening in spite of God.

At first sight the theory attracts: it appears to leave room for a consistent God of Love. But of course it creates more difficulties than it appears to solve. To omit all other criticism, were the theory true, then the Cross must remain an essentially beastly thought. But to leave it like that is to find yourself at once out of your depth, in the meaning of half the hymns you are asked to sing. With one accord these hymns claim the Cross as an essentially healing thought, and become meaningless in this modern setting. The religion of many men today is all out of joint because they will not even begin to face this doctrine.

Let us then consider something of the necessity of the Cross: the worth of the Cross: the place of the Cross: if only the vaguest glimpse of why a God of Love may have 'allowed it'. And we will try very hard to keep away from 'theological language'.

'I, if I be lifted up, will draw all men unto me.' Jesus spoke the words, it would seem, just after this problem had been in his mind. No one can read the preceding passage without realizing the conflict had been real for him. Till this point in his ministry, he had spoken only to his own people — the House of Israel, foreshadowing again and again the principle of the Cross. If they did not seem to understand, we must never forget that in the mind of the Jews a man crucified was a man accursed. Now (John

12:20). with the literal Cross already imminent, come the Greeks — the sages — who always were open to new ideas. At the eleventh hour how could any one hope to convince them of a principle so new and so apparently 'foolish'? The only thing they were likely to witness now was the Cross itself, without background, without explanation. How could they hope to understand? 'Now is my soul troubled. What am I to say? . . . Yet for this cause came I to this hour . . . I, if I be lifted up, will draw all men with me.'

Jesus knows that somehow the Cross itself — for all its stark perplexity — will bring men to the Gospel. He looks into the future, and in faith foresees a universal appeal in the Cross, however little men may know the long history of Israel that was its background. It will appeal to the Greeks, to everybody. He determines to go on.

If, then, we can concentrate on this text, perhaps we may see two or three ways in which the Cross does strangely attract all men. As one approaches it this way, I think there does emerge a dim understanding of the sense in which it was necessary.

In the first place, difficult as it is to find words for it, there is a universal appeal in any kind of cross, that you cannot explain. You can only feel it. Men may rebel at theology, but they cannot deny their own experiences, and in other realms than the strictly religious, what we may describe as an experience of the Cross does inevitably thrill men. It is as if God, having put it at the centre of the world's mystery, also put it into the hearts of men to respond to that Cross. All men respond to crosses.

A great violinist was once playing a solo at a Munich concert, and he played magnificently. I suppose, if there had been no mishap, his artistry would have been appreciated by the musical people there. But in the middle of his solo one of his strings broke — and he finished the piece on three strings. When he came to the end, not just the music-lovers, but every one rose to their feet in an ecstasy of applause. Musical appreciation is not given to every one, but every one is somehow drawn by any man who goes on to the end in face of difficulty. Milton's *Paradise Lost* does not appeal to all. But Milton, going on composing in his blindness, writing when that blow struck him:

> . . . I argue not
> Against Heaven's hand or will, not bate a jot
> Of heart or hope, but still bear up
> And steer right onward.

. . . The appeal of Milton is universal. Getting music out of what is left of life; being stricken with blindness and yet continuing to see supremest visions; fighting a duel with a sword — and when the sword gets broken, fighting on with the hilt: carrying on the same task — in any sphere — more brilliantly when the untoward happens and the crisis comes. Whenever we get a clean-cut example of undiscouraged pluck, it reaches down into our hearts to make music — sweeter than all stories of success — and strikes a reverberating chord that we know is true, explain it as we may.

God, having put a Cross at the centre of the world's mystery, also put it into men's hearts to respond to crosses.

It is here that we see the first — if not the main — purpose of why God may have let it happen. Christ always preached self-sacrifice in his life, and not only in his death. But the Cross, coming at the end, stands clear cut and incisive, reflecting, as in some brilliant miniature, the larger framework of his whole life's message. His life from start to finish was like a sun giving warmth to all who came within its rays; but in his Cross that same sun became focused, as through a lens, till the warmth of his example becomes so concentrated as to set on fire all that it touches. That resolute persistency, the doing battle with the hilt when his sword was gone . . . attracts men, draws them, thrills them. You cannot say why; it is just that it does. In being lifted up from the earth, he arrested the attention not of the House of Israel only, who knew his claims. He moved the universal heart of man.

Very often in the fields of Italy you find a stone monument, or a tombstone, to commemorate some man who died, or some battle that was won. On it is inscribed the legend, and always, at the top, you find in bolder letters, *'STA VIATOR'*, 'Halt, you passer-by, and read this story.' But for that clear-cut word, the traveller might pursue his way regardless of the deed. And the Cross stands as the universal STA VIATOR, for lack of which the world would have missed the story of this Man. It arrests with an action that appeals to the universal heart, saying: 'Read on about this Man who voluntarily did so strange a thing.'

But that, of course, is not all. We might call that the outer circle of attraction: the circle of first attraction that draws men from whatsoever corner of the earth they come. Once a man is arrested there inevitably he becomes drawn to an inner circle of attraction, a deeper circle, of a redder hue. It is as you come here that you glimpse through to the infinite value of what once seemed the biggest obstacle — that it was the perfect, well-beloved Son of God who was crucified. So far we are no

more than life's wayfarer appealed to by this Man. But like all
wayfarers, we cannot travel far along the road of life without
striking the most bitter universal problem of mankind — the
problem of undeserved suffering. Even those for whom the
problem has not yet arisen for themselves must be blind indeed if
they have not witnessed it in others. A man who goes to prison
on a false charge: a woman struck with paralysis when her
children need her most . . . Why on earth should it happen to
these people? But what listener is there who has not thought
already of an instance for himself?

Well, our wayfarer, burdened with this problem, now
confronts the Cross. As he looks into the circumstances of that
Cross, does there not begin to emerge something even more
deeply appealing in its message? As he studies the life of Christ,
whatever other glaring instance he may know of undeserved
suffering, does any even dimly resemble this one? Never was there
a more appalling contrast between what a man deserved and what
he got. Hatred, mockery, betrayal, for Christ, of all people.
Wrongful accusations; illegal law proceedings; death; for a Man
who knew no sin, and in whom no guile was found. Nails, hard
and rusty, driven through the hands and feet of Jesus of
Nazareth. No human language can begin to express the horror of
the discrepancy between what he deserved and what he got. But
do you see how the very horror does not revolt us as one might
expect, but by some Divine transmutation begins to comfort us?
It may not explain things, but it does something else. Before his
sufferings our own pale into insignificance, but do you see what
emerges from that? Why, right down in that deep pit of a
problem of undeserved suffering — in which, when men find
themselves, they think they are forgotten of God — we find, of all
people, Christ. If you like to say so, we find him deeper down in
that pit. And what do we find him doing there? We find him still
going on believing that God is good and that God is ruling! We
find him going on to the bitter end still calling the God who
allowed it his Father. 'Father,' was his dying last breath, 'into thy
hands I commit my spirit.'

'The only man who can help me,' said a man just released from
prison on an unjustified charge, 'is someone who has been in the
hell that I have been in.' And the wonder of the Gospel is, that
there is such a one. But it is the very horror of the Cross that
enables us to say that. It needed a Cross to do it. It is the very
fact that he has borne our griefs and carried our sorrows and has
himself faced the enigma of the Divine Providence, at its most

inexplicable point, that attracts men, every kind of man, in every kind of misfortune, however terrible. With the world as it is, and Divine Providence the mystery that it is, it seems that nothing less than·a Cross could do it. Without this flaming witness of the possibilities of faith, men might indeed be justified in rebelling at the affirmation that the God of this world is also a Father. Magnetic in his sympathy by reason of his Cross, he encourages all men — however miserable their lesser plights — to go on believing that God is good.

Lastly, it is when we get here, only whan we get drawn into this inner circle, that we begin to catch the reflection of the central light that shines from the Cross — to see God face to face. Only when we get here that we may begin to understand the central message of the Cross! Strange and awful as it is, the central message is about God himself. The two approaches we have been considering might be called the human lessons that it needed a Cross to teach. At the outer circle, by the way he went right on, Jesus revealed the height of courage to which humanity can rise in union with God. At the inner circle it is still a human lesson that is presented. He reveals the height of faith to which man can rise faced with the awful mystery of the Divine Providence. But the final lesson of the Cross is not a revelation of what man can be like in relation with the Father, but the revelation of what God is eternally like in relation to his children. For this too, horror of horrors, a Cross was necessary. But it is the other way round. It is God on the Cross this time. Somehow, in the mystery of the Incarnation, it is God on the Cross. For that is the Christian Faith.

Young people to-day cannot have it both ways. If you insist on making your own theology, you must not complain that Christianity does not satisfy you. If you insist that Jesus was 'only a man' and that the Church has been wrong in 'wrapping him up in mystery and calling him Divine,' then you must bear the consequences of a faith that may well mean little or nothing at all. But you must realize that the faith which fails you is a faith of your own construction.

The Church believes, and has always taught, that Christ was God on earth. God took flesh (became incarnate) and dwelt among men. Men may reject belief in, but they cannot elude, the fact that Christ claimed to represent the Father in some unique sense. He claimed that he was Divine. 'He that hath seen me hath seen the Father,' he said to Philip. 'The word that I speak unto you, I speak not of myself, it is the Father that speaks.' 'He that seeth me, seeth not me, but him that sent me.' 'I and the Father are one.' As you read the life of Christ, you may find it difficult to accept, but you cannot escape the fact that in some sense Christ himself claimed to be God. In some sense, then, God was on the Cross. The Pharisees were right at least in the clear-cut problem they made of it. Either he was speaking the truth, or else he spoke the greatest blasphemy that can pass the lips of a sane man. The Pharisees believed it was the greatest blasphemy. We believe it was true. That somehow, in the mystery, here was God on earth: that his whole life was the message of God to man: and that his death was but the last syllable of that great utterance. 'God spoke through the Cross.' Christ, as the representative of God on earth, let himself be crucified, as the only way of showing men what sin costs to God: the awfulness of the pain of sin to God. And to show, too, what God's attitude to sinners is. By dying on the Cross Christ reveals that to sin is very like hammering one more nail into his crucified flesh: and he also reveals what is God's answer to that appalling action. What Christ did in effect, in this aspect, was to say: 'I will show what God is like, by going on loving you, whatever you do to me.' Having loved his own, he loved them to the end, and even of those who reviled him and spat on him and scourged him and buffeted him, even of those Christ spoke for God, saying. 'You are forgiven because you cannot know what you are doing.'

That is what God is like! And, horror of horrors, it needed a Cross that men might really see the enormity of their conduct in face of a God like that.

How does it affect men? How does it change men? What is this healing power that comes from the Cross that all these hymns keep on trying to express? May we say that the Cross was a dramatization — terrible in its reality — of the parable of the Prodigal Son? As we read that story of the son who went into a far country and spent his substance in riotous living, and on his return (only because he was hungry!) found the great unconditional welcome — is there any one who doubts but that that son, when he learnt what his father was really like, surrendered, and accepted those new clothes, and lived at last in freedom in his father's house? Once he had grasped it, could he do aught else than be healed by a love like that?

And what if the Cross is a dramatization of that which is eternally true? What if God is really like that, here and now?

Can we really go on being like this?

And it needed a Cross to tell us that God is like that.

MACLEOD OF FUINARY

Was Jesus resurrected in body or in spirit?

The earliest *written* account (written before the accounts in the Gospels, though these may reflect a much earlier oral tradition, a fact often overlooked) that we have of our Lord's resurrection, and its implications for us, is in St. Paul's first letter to the Corinthians, the fifteenth chapter. There he says: 'I delivered unto you that which also I received, how that Christ died for our sins according to the Scriptures; and that he was buried; and that he hath been raised on the third day according to the Scriptures; and that he appeared to Cephas [Peter] then to the twelve; and then he appeared to above five hundred brethren at once, of whom the greater part remain until now, but some are fallen asleep; then he appeared to James; then to all the Apostles; and last of all, as unto one born out of due time, he appeared to me also.'

Then he goes on to say what some people were then saying, and what many say today (it's not a new notion), that there is no resurrection of the dead. And he declares: 'If there is no resurrection of the dead, neither hath Christ been raised. And if Christ hath not been raised, then is our preaching vain [i.e. of no value] and your faith also is vain . . . If in this life only we have hoped in Christ, we are of all men most pitiable.'

The resurrection of our Lord, then, was clearly for St. Paul the foundation of his faith and preaching. Take it away, he says, and you have nothing left. And that still remains true. Thus some theologians (not generally very remarkable ones) have talked themselves out of belief in the resurrection, and it is not really surprising that some should add that God is dead — though it is pleasant to think that they themselves remain alive, an interesting paradox apparently unperceived by them.

The remainder of this notable chapter is St. Paul's explication of what is involved in our Lord's resurrection, and among others he raises the question of how the dead are raised up and in what kind of body. He goes on to point out that it is not the same body that is raised but another of a different kind that shall be, not terrestial but celestial, using words that of necessity are not definitions but that point beyond themselves to this enthralling mystery which can be grasped only by faith (like the 'above' which no man hath seen at any time, for even physical science, as Einstein reminded us, is a fabric of assumptions and concepts, not 'facts'). Thus he says of the resurrection body: 'It is sown in corruption; it is raised in incorruption: it is sown in dishonour; it is raised in glory: it is sown in weakness; it is raised in power: it is sown a natural body; it is raised a spiritual body.'

As so many have noted, these words have been variously interpreted, and the interpretations fall mainly into three groups.

There is first, the widely held view in the early Church, and indeed probably generally throughout its history (and thought to be supported by the Gospel narratives, especially those which represent certain physical aspects of our Lord's resurrection appearings) that our Lord's resurrection (and so accordingly in due course will ours be) was a *revivication of the physical body*, very similar to that of Lazarus. This notion has led to much confusion in thought and to much asperity in debate — usually with the debaters talking not to, but past each other.

Secondly, it is often suggested, in various forms, that our Lord's resurrection was *of the spirit only*, and the persistence of this notion is reflected in many Christian funeral services where the emphasis is on the 'soul'. This idea is derived perhaps chiefly from some Greek or even Hebrew thought which often speaks of the immortality of the soul, conveying this idea if not always in these precise words. This is expressly repudiated in St. Luke's Gospel, often airily dismissed as a 'late' account, when it would be of more value not to count the six or seven years between it and St. Mark as of importance, but rather the fact that it is emphasised particularly by the one evangelist with a skilled scientific medical training. 'Why are ye troubled?' he records Jesus as saying, when they were 'terrified and affrighted and supposed that they beheld a spirit'. 'See my hands and my feet, that it is I myself: handle me, and see, for a spirit hath not flesh and bones, as ye behold me having.' If we accept the New Testament accounts it is clear that they all have this in common, that the resurrection of our Lord is there described as a 're-appearance of his total personality', which includes the bodily expression of his being. This is so evident that he can be recognized in a way which is more than the manifestation of a bodiless 'spirit' (Tillich).

Again, a theory often put forward in some form may be classified as a *psychological* one — that is, that it did not happen, but was merely thought to have happened. It was an event in the disciples' minds, a dream or a vision, or even a hope at first invented, then eventually believed to be true, and in 'later narratives' arising within the Christian community given concrete support even to the inclusion of all sorts of physical events. Such a theory is, of course, difficult to refute — it seems so modern, so 'with it', and is so intangible with nothing to grasp in it. But to believe it we must agree to throw the New Testament overboard, deny the witness of the apostles as self-deluded men, consider the Christian Church to have been founded on a lie, and our faith to be of no value. That is a tall order, and in fact leads nowhere except perhaps to give the holder a sense of self-importance at being so 'advanced' (though the notion is nothing new). There is, we should note in passing, nothing by which this view can be rationally proved to be true. It is a mere assumption, and therefore is grasped not by reason but by faith. As most of those who hold this view pride themselves on being rationalists, it may be thought odd to see them in faith clinging irrationally to guesses clear against the testimony of eye-witnesses.

It is also, one may mention, general practice among defenders of any of these theories, and others as well, to point out that what we have in the resurrection narratives is the fulfilment of a belief already fixed in the disciples' minds. They expected him, and so he came or they thought he came. This is indeed the opposite of the facts. They didn't expect him. They thought all was lost. They had hoped that it would be 'he that would redeem Israel'. But the crucifixion dashed these hopes. Though he had said he would rise again, they did not grasp the possibility. They hid away, fearful and afraid, and without hope.

Then, we read, he *came.* That was the startling and unexpected fact that aroused faith in them. The resurrection was not created by faith, but faith was re-created by the resurrection. The fact of resurrection was not an act of faith, but a mighty act of God. 'This Jesus whom *ye* crucified' they proclaimed, '*God* hath raised up'.

Thus the New Testament proclaims that Jesus came in a total but also new way. He was raised a 'spiritual body' says St. Paul, groping for words. These can be dismissed by a superficial analysis, but we then brush aside the profound fact St. Paul is struggling to convey and which the New Testament asserts, namely, that these theories mentioned above are all wrong and that our Lord's resurrection is a manifestation of something new, not one of revivification of a dead body, or immortality of the soul, or the projection of pious hopes, but the proof of a new and richer existence, continuous with this present one, but 'changed', 'glorified', 'transfigured'. And a little reflection indeed suggests that this is wholly rational and in accord with all the New Testament statements, and an assertion capable of creating in us a responding and eager hope as it did for the first disciples. Here we are confronted by One whom we can call Master, Lord and Leader, and who alone can give our life full meaning. He became not just a remembered hero inspiring devotion, but a living, commanding, and saving Lord. Death was real — we all must face it — but its power is now broken; it has been by him, and now can be through him, defeated. Thus 'life', we come to see in him, is not a perpetuation of this existence for ever (a really dreadful thought, if we reflect upon it) but entrance through the dark gate of death into a new and transformed existence of a different quality, incredible in its richness and possibilities. Yet there is continuity also, for our present existence has meaning too, if a limited meaning. This is related in the event of the empty tomb, where by a mysterious act of God the old body is caught up, dissolved, and transfigured into the new existence 'white and shining' continuous with the old, yet transformed.

Such, in brief, is what the resurrection of our Lord means to me. To receive this belief is an act of faith, but not of blind faith, an act of faith not contradicted but confirmed by reason; it is a reasonable faith. It is based upon the New Testament assertions and narratives, explaining them but not explaining them away. It is based upon the experience of the first disciples. It is based upon the continuous and triumphant existence of the Church, while all Kingdoms have fallen and perished. It is based upon personal experience of a gripping and saving kind. In it I can rest, rejoice, and obey.

It is a conviction also continually renewed by the experience of obedience; by the study of Holy Scripture; by a growing sense of the profound reality of prayer; and finally (and this should be often) by participation of the Lord's Supper where we experience anew his life poured forth in victory when he is made known to us, as to those in Emmaus, in the breaking of bread. Thus every Communion is a joyous Easter, a receiving of and surrender to the living Christ, so that he is in us and we in him. For me our Lord's resurrection gives my life and other lives meaning, direction, and hope; and invests life with a quality of daily obedience to divine Love, in me imperfectly fulfilled but thrilling in its power, transforming in its impact.

W. D. MAXWELL

Does the resurrection of the body mean the survival of the soul?

Questions are sometimes so framed that 'Yes' and 'No' are both equally likely to be misleading (as with the classic example, 'Have you stopped beating your wife?'). The question before us is of this sort. But if one had to give an unqualified 'Yes' or 'No', the position implied by the New Testament would be better represented by 'No' than by 'Yes': No, the resurrection of the body does not mean the same thing as the survival of the soul.[1]

But, that being said, this 'No' needs to be explained and qualified, if this position is not to be misunderstood; and if, in the end, the reader feels that this answer has (in a well-known phrase[2]) 'suffered death by a thousand qualifications', that may mean, not that Christians don't know their mind, but that — like most really important matters — this is a delicate and difficult subject. Readers are invited to go on to study a fuller account of the biblical position in O. Cullmann's lively little book *Immortality of the Soul or Resurrection of the Dead?*[3]

In this answer, which chooses 'the resurrection of the body'[4] in preference to 'the immortality of the soul', the resurrection of the body is not to be understood to mean a crudely material reconstitution of the body. Perhaps it will clarify the matter if we ask what the phrase is trying to safeguard. A reluctance to speak of the survival of the soul is dictated by two positive convictions, the first related to the word 'survival' and the second to the word 'soul'. The first conviction is that human beings are dependent on God for life: they are not inherently, or in their own right, immortal or indestructible or able to 'survive'. The second conviction is that a person cannot be divided into 'soul' and 'body'. A person *is* a living body, rather than some other thing living inside a body. He may say 'My head aches' or 'My arm is broken' but he will not say 'My body is hurt': he will say 'I am hurt'. If, now, we put the two convictions into a single sentence, we shall have to say something like this: If a person does have any life beyond death, it will be because his entire self has been transformed or renewed by God, not because a detachable part of himself is inherently indestructible and has escaped from the perishable remainder and survived. The first conviction concerns man's relation towards God, as created and as dependent on God the Creator: the second concerns man's individuality, and represents a unitary, 'monistic' view of it, as contrasted with a 'dualistic' view.[5]

But here the answer just given runs into heavy weather in two respects. (i) First, nobody can deny that, at death, what we ordinarily call the body does decay. Therefore, if we insist on the indivisibility and unity of a person, is he not demonstrably done for at death? *He* (on this showing) is visibly decaying. Alternatively, if we still insist on the reality of life after death, are we not driven, after all, to some sort of dualism, and compelled to say that something other than the body has survived? And, if so, is not the time-honoured word for that something 'the soul', as contrasted with 'the body'? How often a moralist must have said things like, 'Remember, you have an immortal soul!' The answer implied by the New Testament as a whole is to insist, indeed, on the unity and indivisibility of the personality, which means approving the use of the word 'body' for a whole person; but to postulate also that the material body which decays is not the only conceivable sort of body: why should it not be replaced by, or turned into, some other mode of self-expression equally deserving of the term 'body'? In other words, 'body' is a word which helps to safeguard a full, undiminished personality. The Christian can have no objection to using the word 'soul' if it is explained to mean a total person who, during his 'mortal' life organizes material particles so as to express himself, and may thereafter become capable of expressing himself in some other medium. A common formula of Christian prayer, reflecting a view widely held by Christians, is for 'the souls of the departed'. But it would be less misleading and closer to the implications of biblical thought to pray simply for 'the departed' — the point being that the idea of a self-existent 'soul' — an immortal something — merely encased in a mortal body is alien to the general tenor of the Bible, and endangers both the idea of full personhood, and the Christian doctrine of creation, which requires a positive, not an escapist, attitude towards matter and insists on the ideal of using matter, as part of God's good creation, not trying to escape from it. Thus, while it seems necessary to distinguish the material particles from the 'self' which uses them and expresses itself in them, the fact remains that the self, nevertheless, does use them and does exist in and through them as long as they are being thus used; and the self cannot be separated, absolutely, from the total resulting organism at any given moment. But, if so, then such a self may still reasonably be spoken of as a body, even when, subsequently, it participates in some other mode of existence, using a different and a non-material medium of self-expression.

In the New Testament, the classic passage concerned with this question is 1 Cor. 15. There, admittedly, Paul uses analogies which no longer hold. He appeals to the belief that different kinds of 'flesh' or stuff go to the making, respectively, of beasts, birds, fishes, and (an addition which, to the modern mind, is simply quaint) stars. If so, then — so Paul's argument runs — it is conceivable that a 'body' made of material stuff in this life may be made of different stuff in some other existence. Similarly, and rather more pertinently, Paul appeals to the difference that exists — yet without loss of identity — between a seed and the plant that grows from it. But this is scarcely convincing; for we can see that, however great a range of material manifestations there may be, within the world of matter, as between species and species and (in an individual of one species) between one phase and another, this is still no more than a remote analogy to any change that may be postulated between two different worlds of existence — a material and a non-material world; and we are still left without any direct evidence of the reality of the latter.

What is fundamental, however, in 1 Cor. 15, is the twofold belief to which allusion has already been made. First, there is this belief about the material world as created by God with a purpose. The consequence of this belief is to recognize matter as a real, if temporary, part of a person's self-expression, and as something to be used and transformed rather than escaped from. And, secondly, there is the belief that God alone is the source of life, so that it is only because he has given us life that we are alive now, and only if he gives us new life that we shall live hereafter.

This has brought us to (ii), the second respect in which the answer here adopted runs into difficulties. This answer (to recapitulate what has just been said), having stressed the unity and continuity of the person (using the term 'body' to safeguard this conviction), goes on to say, with an apparent contradiction, that there is, after all, no *inherent* continuity. The continuity, it says, depends entirely on God. If there is life for me beyond this mortal phase, it will only be because God continues to hold me in life. When Jesus was challenged by the Sadducees, who did not believe in life after death,[6] he did not reply by appealing to a division between a mortal body and an immortal soul, or to apocalyptic mythology about the after-life: he appealed, instead, to God's initiative in entering into dialogue with man. If God calls himself Abraham's God, then Abraham is alive. Life depends not on any inherent survival-power of the human self, as though man were essentially an indestructible, immortal soul, but on God's call. Thus, life is a dialogue with God. Death is a real full-stop, and only if God speaks the next sentence will there be continued life for us. Well, but if so, where — it may be asked — do the Christian doctrines of responsibility, of judgment, and of heaven and hell come in? That is the second difficulty. Are we not, by making man thus completely dependent on God, denying his personal responsibility and his continued existence until he comes to stand his trial before the eternal judgment seat and to be sentenced accordingly? Are we not subscribing, by implication, to an arbitrary form of 'conditional immortality' — annihilation for some, life for others? Besides, many persons would say that so-called psychic phenomena, as well as the observation of the extent to which 'mind' seems to be able to triumph over 'matter', prompt them to believe in survival even for those who seem unresponsive to God. By that doctrine of the divine 'dialogue' and the utter dependence of man on God, are we not denying the evident vitality and responsibility and dignity of human nature?

Perhaps the most consistent answer to this objection is to reaffirm indeed that a person's existence depends on God's call, but to affirm also that God, in his mercy, refuses to be silenced by a man's unresponsiveness; and that, although man is free to reject him, God in actual fact, goes on calling, even when he is rejected. God holds us in life; and, although theoretically it is death for us if we ultimately persist in our refusal to respond, yet it is inconceivable that God's love will ever give up. In other words, it seems right to affirm that it is only because of God's call that we live at all; but also to dare to believe that God's call does not cease, so long as there is any human person to address. This, without robbing man of his responsibility — which can only be adequately described in terms of choosing heaven or hell — affirms that God's love is undefeatable.

At any rate — even supposing we had to allow that there must be a point beyond which there can be no return — it is worth observing that there is no reason to regard physical death as the moment of eternal fixation of a person's condition. If life depends not on any inherent immortality in us but on God's call, it does not follow that God's call ceases at physical death. There are small grounds for limiting the processes of entering life or retreating from life, obeying or refusing God, to this mortal life alone. It is hardly convincing simply to quote 'You will die in your sins' (John 8:24), or to interpret the story of the rich man and Lazarus (Luke 16:19ff) as meant to be a considered, authoritative statement on this question. Thus, the scope of God's call cannot convincingly be limited to our time—space existence, nor a term set to the scope and duration of God's love. On the other hand, neither is there any way of describing the ultimate gravity of man's responsibility and free personhood, except in terms of eternal gain and loss, of heaven and hell. To turn from God *is* hell (whether in this life or beyond it), and the fact that God goes on calling us makes us alive enough to experience hell as long as we do not respond to him. But if we have to use terms of heaven and hell to describe the reality and gravity of man's choice, we have to use terms of endless undefeatability to describe the scope of God's almighty love: here, what can we say, but that he goes on patiently calling till we do respond? There is no denying that there are passages in the New Testament such as Rom. 1:28, declaring that God 'gives up' those who give him up; but is it right to understand these as descriptions of God's character, and not rather of man's awful responsibility? In other words, recognizing to the full all that the Bible says about eternal judgment, must we not also recognize that it describes God's character as such that his concern for man is absolute? Perhaps, therefore, we are forced to affirm two contradictory sets of terms (the one descriptive of human responsibility, the other of the love of God) and hold them in tension.

Returning, now, to 1 Cor. 15, what is evidentially weighty in it is Paul's appeal to the facts about Jesus. Jesus had been put to death, and he had been buried; yet, a large number of witnesses claimed to have subsequently seen him alive. And the sort of life that he now possessed was, they were convinced, not a mortal, terminable life, nor one that belonged to the dimensions of this world. This conviction is evident from the fact that nowhere in the traditions is there a trace of a suggestion that this aliveness of Jesus was terminated a second time. (Note how the different Gospels end.) Paul was only putting into words the implications of the traditions when he said, 'Christ, once raised from among the dead, is never to die again. Death no longer has authority over him. The death that he died, he died to sin once and for all; the life that he lives, he lives to God.' (Rom. 6:9f.) Something must have happened, to create this conviction. There was apparently nothing in the current beliefs of Pharisaic Judaism to suggest it, for, even if the Pharisees hoped for a transcendental life for righteous Jews after history had been wound up, there seems to have been nothing in their beliefs to dispose them to expect a similar transcendental aliveness for one individual while time still continued. Still less is there anything in Zoroastrianism (to which appeal is sometimes made) to account for this idea. Thus there is a case which it is difficult to ignore for postulating some exceptional 'act of God' to explain the genesis of this conviction. The Christian word for this act is the resurrection of Jesus from among the dead. And the conclusion is that he must have shown himself alive to his friends, if their conviction is to be accounted for.

The stories of the appearances of Jesus do not stand or fall with the stories of the empty tomb, and these latter are often deemed comparatively late and legendary. But it is arguable that, on the contrary, they are early and doctrinally significant. There is little or nothing in them that is demonstrably late or secondary; and doctrinally it may be that they fit in, in some such way as follows. If the transcendental aliveness of Jesus after death anticipated, as it were, the end of time, bringing the ultimate in some sense inside the temporal, then perhaps, in the transformation of his material body into a 'body' of a different kind, Jesus may also have anticipated some ultimate plan of God for using up matter into what is trans-material. And, if so, then Christians, whose material particles do disintegrate at death and are dispersed (dramatically and horribly when death occurs through an explosion or the like, but equally surely even in natural death), may yet be believed to have begun the process, in their lifetime, of using up matter into something more permanent; and it may be God's intention that ultimately the whole of matter should be thus transformed. The total transformation of Jesus indicated by the empty tomb would then be a sort of harbinger. If we believe in creation 'out of nothing', is there any reason why that which was created should not be used up 'into something' new? Fuel is transformed into energy. May not human personality be enabled, by God's vitality, to turn matter into something permanent, and may not what Paul calls 'a spiritual body' be the beginning of this process for each individual? The matter which is manifestly 'left behind' at death may yet be intended to become part of some such transformation ultimately.

If you refer again to the New Testament this seems compatible with 1 Cor. 15; and in 2 Cor. 4:7 — 5:10, Paul seems to be saying that the positive acceptance and use, in the name of Jesus, of all the wear and tear of mortality is the way in which, by God's grace and under his direction, we are enabled to receive a 'heavenly dwelling'. Instead of meeting the mortality, the *necrosis*, with which we are saddled, with resentment or attempting to evade it, we can affirm it as 'the *necrosis* of Jesus' (2 Cor. 4:10). It is the very mortality which Jesus affirmed and used — used up into new life. And, using it ourselves in his name as the present, temporary medium through which to perform the will of God, we may thus be enabled by God to begin at once to enter upon a new and permanent existence (2 Cor. 5:1—5).

This, to sum up, Paul can distinguish two different modes of existence as that of the merely animal body and that of the spiritual body (1 Cor. 15:44); and he can speak of living on 'in the flesh' (Phil. 1:22) when he means continuing in the present mode of existence. And behind this sort of terminology is the recognition that the real issue is not (as with dualism) between the material and the immaterial but between failing to respond to God and his will and responding to him and doing his will. The crucial question is not 'Am I in the flesh or am I an emancipated, disembodied soul?' but 'Am I a "body" which rejects God or one which obeys his will?' Am I (in Paul's striking phrase in 2 Cor 10:3), though necessarily '*in* flesh', yet not living '*according* to flesh' (i.e. not living in such a way as to capitulate to the material by immorality instead of controlling and using it for God's will)? If I am obeying God — using matter in line with his design — then God will continue my selfhood beyond physical death, I shall be using matter up into something more permanent. But if I am rejecting God and living 'according to the flesh' (letting the material use me), then I am in the most important sense already facing in the direction of death.

It is along some such lines as these that the explanation may be found of what might seem, at first, to be a perverse insistence in such Christian traditions as have kept close to biblical viewpoints, on the resurrection of the body rather than the immortality of the soul.

C. F. D. MOULE

1 The statement which follows is not intended to be a representative survey of the history of Christian opinion on this matter up to the present day. It is simply one student's understanding of the implications of certain passages in the New Testament itself.

2 Used by A. G. N. Flew, in *New Essays in Philosophical Theology*, edd. A. G. N. Flew and A. MacIntyre (London, S.C.M. Press, 1955), p.107.

3 London, Epworth Press, 1958; reprinted in K. Stendahl (ed.), *Immortality and Resurrection: Death in the Western World: Two Conflicting Currents of Thought* (New York, Macmillan Co., 1965).

4 'The resurrection of the flesh' occurs in certain 'creeds' and other ancient documents, but is not in line with the New Testament, and ought never to have been introduced.

5 The New Testament is by no means consistent in its terminology, and there are certainly 'dualistic' phrases. See, e.g., Mark 14:38, 'the spirit is willing but the flesh is weak'; 1 Cor. 5:3, 'absent in body, present in spirit'; 1 Thess. 5:23, 'your whole spirit and soul and body'; 3 John 2, 'I pray that you may prosper and be in health, just as your soul is prospering'. But the whole trend of New Testament thought is in the monistic direction, and it is difficult to make sense of the Pauline epistles on any other basis.

6 Mark 12:18 ff. (Matt. 22:23 ff.; Luke 20:27 ff.)

7 *Necrosis* (from *necros*, dead body) is the Greek word used by Paul in 2 Cor. 4:10, 'bearing about in the body the dying (*necrosis*) of the Lord Jesus' (A.V.).

Bibliography

The following suggestions 'For Further Reading' are listed by Professor Mascall in connection with his contribution 'How can you prove that God exists?'. The plan of this book does not allow for bibliographies to individual articles, but this list, on such an important subject, is printed here for all those who wish to pursue the matter. Its contents are relevant to several other articles besides Professor Mascall's own.

GENERAL

'The Vindication of Religion', by A. E. Taylor, in *Essays Catholic and Critical,* edited by E. G. Selwyn. An excellent brief survey.
He Who Is, by E. L. Mascall. Systematic and traditional.
Our Knowledge of God, by John Baillie. Concise, with a stress on experience.
Our Experience of God, by H. D. Lewis. Wide ranging and comprehensive.
God-Talk, by John Macquarrie. Discusses much contemporary thinking.
The Christian Knowledge of God, by H. P. Owen. A splendid up-to-date and most readable discussion.
God and Philosophy, by E. Gilson. Brief, pungent and cogent.

THE ONTOLOGICAL ARGUMENT

The Ontological Argument, edited by A. Plantinga. Contains all the chief texts from Anselm to the present day, clearly arranged and introduced.
The Many-faced Argument, edited by A. G. McGill and John Hick. A large collection of essays, excellent but not for the beginner.

THE COSMOLOGICAL ARGUMENT

Finite and Infinite, by A. M. Farrer. Massive and systematic; needs application, but repays it.

THE PROBLEM OF EVIL

Love Almighty and Ills Unlimited, by A. M. Farrer. Concise, and faces the problem honestly.
The Problem of Pain, by C. S. Lewis. Also concise and honest.
Evil and the God of Love, by John Hick. The best modern discussion; large but very readable.

THE TELEOLOGICAL ARGUMENT

Philosophical Theology, by F. R. Tennant. A classic, in two large volumes, somewhat dated but still impressive.
Nature, Man and God, by William Temple. Referred to in the text above.
A Science of God? by A. M. Farrer. Brief but very impressive and thoroughly contemporary.

THE MORAL ARGUMENT

The Moral Argument for Christian Theism, by H. P. Owen. Compact but comprehensive. The best modern book on the subject.
The Faith of a Moralist, by A. E. Taylor. Two large volumes. Readable and untechnical.

The above are only a small selection from the great mass of books available.

Appendix
Contents of Part II

*Index of Contributors
to Parts I and II
with biographical notes*

E. P. Dickie, M.C., D.D., LL.D., Emeritus Professor of Divinity, St. Andrews University. . . . . *Part I, p.* 120
An Extra-Chaplain to H.M. the Queen in Scotland.

David L. Edwards, M.A., Canon of Westminster and Rector of St. Margaret's since 1970. . . . . *Part II, p.* 49
Formerly Fellow and Dean of King's College, Cambridge.

Rosemary Haughton, R.C. Author, Broadcaster and Lecturer. *Part I, p.* 113

Martin Jarrett-Kerr, M.A., C.R., Member of Community of the Resurrection, Mirfield, since 1943; Warden, Hostel of the Resurrection, Leeds. . . . . *Part II, p.* 102
Formerly Vice-Principal of the College of the Resurrection, Mirfield, and then of the College of the Resurrection, Rosettenville, South Africa.

Daniel Jenkins, D.D., Chaplain, University of Sussex. . . *Part II, p.* 23
Formerly Minister of the King's Weigh House, London.

Geoffrey W. H. Lampe, M.C., D.D., F.B.A., Regius Professor of Divinity, Cambridge University, since 1970; Fellow of Gonville and Caius College, Cambridge. . . . . *Part I, p.* 70
Formerly Professor of Theology and Vice-Principal, Birmingham University, and Ely Professor of Divinity, Cambridge.

Sir Bernard Lovell, O.B.E., D.Sc., LL.D., F.R.S., Professor of Radio Astronomy, Manchester University, since 1951. . *Part II, p.* 18

Geddes MacGregor, LL.B., D.Phil., D.D., F.R.S.L., Distinguished Professor of Philosophy, Southern California University, since 1966, and Canon Theologian of St. Paul's Cathedral, Los Angeles, since 1968.
Part II, p. 62
Formerly Minister of Trinity Church, Glasgow (Church of Scotland).

John McIntyre, D.Litt., D.D., Professor of Divinity, Edinburgh University, since 1956 and Principal of New College, Edinburgh, since 1968.
Part I, p. 10
Formerly Professor of Theology and Principal of St. Andrew's College, University of Sydney.

Lord MacLeod of Fuinary, Bart., M.C., D.Litt., D.D., LL.D., Founder of the Iona Community. Hon. Fellow, Oriel College, Oxford. An Extra-Chaplain to H.M. the Queen in Scotland. . *Part I, p.* 141
Formerly Minister of St. Cuthbert's, Edinburgh, and Govan, Glasgow, and Moderator of the General Assembly of the Church of Scotland, 1957-58.

C. F. D. Moule, D.D., F.B.A., Lady Margaret's Professor of Divinity, Cambridge University, Fellow of Clare College, Cambridge, Canon Theologian of Leicester. . . . .   *Part I, p.* 151

John Murray, S.J., formerly Professor of the History of Philosophy at Heythorp College, Oxford, and Gregorian University, Rome, and Superior of the Sacred Heart, Edinburgh. . . .   *Part I, p.* 90

William Neil, Ph.D., D.D., Reader in Biblical Studies, Nottingham University. . . . .   *Part I, p.* 50
Formerly Head of the Department of Biblical Studies, Aberdeen University.

The Rt. Rev. I. T. Ramsey, D.D., Bishop of Durham, Hon. Fellow of Oriel College, Oxford and Christ's College, Cambridge. .   *Part II, p.* 83
Formerly Professor of the Philosophy of the Christian Religion, Oxford University.

The Most Rev. A. M. Ramsey, D.Litt., D.D., D.C.L., Archbishop of Canterbury; Hon. Fellow Magdalene College, Cambridge. *Part II, p.* 107
Formerly Professor of Divinity at Durham University, Regius Professor of Divinity, Cambridge University, Bishop of Durham and Archbishop of York.

J. K. S. Reid, C.B.E., T.D., D.D., Professor of Christian Dogmatics, Aberdeen University since 1961; Secretary of Joint Committee on New Translation of the Bible. . . . .   *Part I, p.* 62
Formerly Professor of Theology, Leeds University.

James S. Stewart, D.D., Emeritus Professor of New Testament, Edinburgh University; an Extra-Chaplain to H.M. the Queen in Scotland.
Part I, p. 106
Formerly Moderator of the General Assembly of the Church of Scotland, 1963-64.

The Rt. Rev. Mervyn Stockwood, D.Litt., D.D., Bishop of Southwark.
Part II, p. 118
Formerly Vicar of Great St. Mary's (University Church), Cambridge, and Hon. Canon of Bristol.

T. F. Torrance, M.B.E., D.Litt., D.D., D.Th., D.Theol., Professor of Christian Dogmatics, Edinburgh University. . .   *Part I, p.* 17
Formerly Professor of Church History, Edinburgh University.

Roland Walls, M.A., Lecturer in Dogmatics, Edinburgh University.
Part I, p. 45
Formerly Chaplain and Dean, Corpus Christi College, Cambridge.

Subject index and glossary

Names of Contributors appear in the Index of Contributors, pages 163–7; titles of contributions to this volume are given in the Contents List, pages xiii–xiv, and of those to Part II in Appendix, pages 161–2.

101186

230
W952
c.2

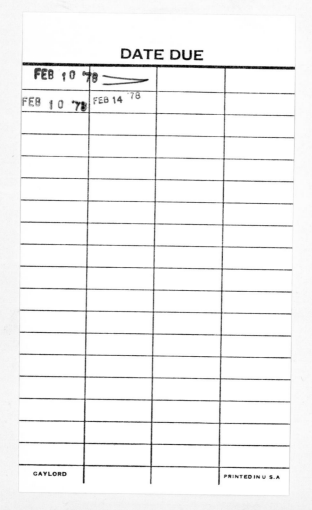

DATE DUE

FEB 10 '78			
FEB 10 '78	FEB 14 '78		
GAYLORD			PRINTED IN U.S.A